# Approac

*A Guide for Worship Leaders
and Worshippers*

Christopher J. Ellis

*with practical exercises by
Anthony Clarke*

CANTERBURY
PRESS
Norwich

First published in 2009 by the Canterbury Press Norwich
Editorial office
13–17 Long Lane,
London, EC1A 9PN, UK

Canterbury Press is an imprint of Hymns Ancient and Modern Ltd
(a registered charity)
St Mary's Works, St Mary's Plain,
Norwich, NR3 3BH, UK

www.scm-canterburypress.co.uk

British Library Cataloguing in Publication data.

A catalogue record for this book is available
from the British Library.

978 1 85311 886 9

Typeset by Regent Typesetting, London
Printed in the UK by
CPI William Clowes, Beccles, NR34 7TL

# Contents

For Marilyn, with love,
and for the students of Bristol Baptist College

# Preface

This book began as a fairly straightforward 'beginner's guide to leading worship' and it flowed from two sources. First, my experience of teaching people the principles of worship, and of encouraging them to develop skills of worship leadership in the free church tradition, which led me to the conviction that such a book was crying out to be written. Second, the production of *Gathering for Worship: Patterns and Prayers for the Community of Disciples* for the Baptist Union of Great Britain (Canterbury Press 2005) which led to further suggestions that such a book be attempted.

But this book changed as it grew. What began as a book of practical instruction soon became a more reflective project in which readers were asked to think through various issues concerning worship. Something which began with the narrow focus of helping potential worship leaders developed into a book about worship which might help any who wanted to learn more about this highest of all callings, the call to worship God.

Before God invites people to become worship leaders, God calls worshippers. We cannot separate leading and worshipping. On the one hand, leaders are called to be worshippers and, on the other hand, the very process of reflecting on the practice of worship leadership will draw us into an exploration of the nature of worship – as well as a seeking after God. A 'how-to-do-it manual' which ignores these higher, and deeper, themes is doomed to failure. Consequently, this book dares to go further and even, if only sometimes, it encourages the reader to go deeper, I will be pleased.

A few sections of what follows began as articles in the *Baptist Times*. I would like to thank its editor, Mark Woods, for his willingness to give permission for their development here. In addition, there are three people I wish to thank. First, the early plans for this project were developed in partnership with Myra Blyth who co-edited *Gathering for Worship* with me. Our discussions were always lively and fruitful. Second, I wish to thank Anthony Clarke for his comments on the text and, especially, for his preparation of the practical exercises which I believe enhance this book and offer the opportunity for readers to become learners. Finally, I wish to thank Marilyn, my wife, not only for her sharing in the leadership of worship, but for her patience and encouragement.

I wish to dedicate this book to the students of Bristol Baptist College whose desire to learn provoked me to develop a course entitled 'The Survivors Guide to Leading Worship'. Much of that course has been incorporated into this book.

Christopher Ellis
*The Feast of Christ the King 2008*

# Beginnings

# So you've been asked to lead worship . . .

So you've been asked to lead worship. Well, it's often not quite so straightforward as that. You may have been asked to lead a whole service, or you may simply have been invited to take part in a service by leading prayers or a sequence of songs. You may have been asked to join the worship team of a local church where you will share in the planning and leading of services. You may have led worship quite often but are now preparing to be an ordained minister. You may be wondering whether you have a gift which can be developed and used in the future. Or you may just be a worshipper and you want to appreciate worship more fully and have picked up this book in the hope that it might broaden and deepen your understanding.

Well, I hope this book will help. It will offer practical guidance on how to plan services, lead prayers and find suitable resources for use in worship. But I hope it will do much more because I want to encourage you to think about worship so that the way you do things is affected by what you think the nature and purpose of worship to be. I don't want to put you off, but there will be some theology and there will be plenty of opportunities for reflection, so that what you do in worship is informed by what you believe.

But I also hope this book will be of help to people who are not expecting to lead worship, and simply see themselves as worshippers. Believe me – there is no higher calling than to be called to worship God. Yes we are all called – but that doesn't change the truth that this should be the summit of our human experience and the central feature of our Christian living. It is true that this book is written in a form which addresses someone who wants to learn how to lead worship. But because this learning happens by thinking about worship, it can also inform and enrich anyone who wishes to deepen their understanding of Christian worship.

## By invitation

Let's get one thing straight at the beginning. We don't set ourselves up as worship leaders. We don't wake up one day and say, 'Oh, I think I'd like to lead worship.' No – we get invited.

This invitation can come in all sorts of ways, but it will often be a request to help out in the congregation in which we usually worship. Perhaps first we are asked to lead some prayers or the opening worship in a service. The point is that the invitation will come from the leadership of the church, whether a minister, or someone with a responsibility for organizing the leading of weekly services. The invitation will usually come because there is a need and because someone has seen in you gifts which they believe can help the church – or at least the possibility of gifts which could be developed in time.

This invitation business is important because when we lead worship we do so as a representative of the church community and we do it in order to serve God through serving the community. We may enjoy the experience or we may be petrified – but we do it knowing that other people have entrusted us with this role. You see, worship is a community activity and so the community, or its representatives, invite and encourage us to participate by using our particular gifts, in this case the gift of leadership.

## Worship is a community thing

Now it's perfectly possible to worship God on your own. You can do it in front of a glorious sunset or you can do it in your own personal prayer time. But the 'worship' which this book is about is the normal use of the word – the worship event which is a gathering together of the church community in order to share in the worship of God.

And whenever there is a gathering of people for a shared purpose, somebody or somebodies will need to lead them. Sometimes it is possible, with a small group, to have very informal worship where nothing is organized beforehand and most things are spontaneous. But even that kind of worship needs a leader who will enable people to contribute in a way that is helpful, constructive and honouring to God. The apostle Paul wrote about God giving different gifts to different people in the church and said that each of those gifts needs to be shared by the person to whom they have been entrusted, and honoured by those entrusted with other gifts in the community. The gift of leadership is very important – whatever the style of worship, whether formal or informal, planned in detail, or largely spontaneous.

## A matter of confidence

So perhaps you're asking, 'Why me?' This is where the invitation of the Christian community and other people's encouragement is so important. You might be very nervous or even think that you are not good enough to undertake such an important task as leading other people in worship. You would be right on both counts! Yes, it is important and none of us is good enough. But if we have been asked by others to lead worship, or help others in doing so, then it may well be that God is speaking to us through them, and the best way to find out is to have a go and continue to listen to others.

> ### Exercise
>
> Write down a brief description of the circumstances which led you to be invited to lead worship, the gifts which others have seen in you, and the challenges you think you will face.
>
> This is part of your journey with God, and it would be good to keep this piece of paper safe, because you might want to look at it again in the future.

In all forms of Christian service, the concept of 'call' is central. For example, I am a minister not because I am good enough or clever enough but because, through other people and through my own heart, God has called me to ministry. We stand up in front of other people because God calls us to the work, not because we deserve some kind of public recognition.

There are usually two dimensions in a call to Christian service. First, there is the external dimension, which includes input and advice from other people as they recognize in you appropriate gifts and a suitable character. I include in this external dimension your own assessment of what you can do or what, through training, you could do. Second, there is the internal dimension of the call – your own sense that this is what you should do or, put another way, what you think God wants you to do.

Both dimensions are important, although they don't necessarily become clear at the same time. Yet a sense of call is vital in enabling us to tackle something which from a human perspective might simply be seen as arrogance or misplaced optimism.

Our confidence comes from the call of God – and even if we are not sure of that call, then to test it by trying is an honourable way to behave. It's a form of living by faith in which we act as though God has called us and wait to see what happens – either there will be a gentle 'No', or there will be encouragement to continue. But even then there will be plenty of work. God gives us gifts, but they are often raw materials which need nurturing and developing through learning, training, practice and reflection. This book is designed to help in that process.

## Variations on a theme

Of course there are different denominations, with differing styles of worship, and there can often be wide variations of worship style within denominations. One book can't help everyone equally, and each author will have their own viewpoint. This particular book is written from the perspective of free church worship, though I hope it will be helpful to a range of people trying to lead worship in different kinds of church. There is something here for the independent charismatic church and for the more traditional free church service. Also, I believe it will have something to offer people from more liturgical traditions, especially with the increasing opportunities in those traditions for local creativity and informality.

## A leading question

But let's return to the question of leadership. Worship leadership is a ministry, a service to God and the people of God. It is not restricted to ordained ministers, though in some denominations some parts of worship can only be led by such people. It is not my intention to argue the case about what can or cannot be done by someone who is not ordained. Nonetheless, a number of free churches will permit someone who is not ordained, for example, to lead a communion service. In order to help in such circumstances, the leading of communion will be included in what follows, but I recognize that for some of my readers that particular chapter may not be as useful as others. However, because I want us to think about why we do certain things and what the meanings of those things

6

might be, I hope that even that chapter will enrich the reader's under-standing of communion, even if they are not going to be leading.

Meanwhile, remember that leadership is a service. Leaders exist in order to serve the people they lead or, more particularly, to enable the group they lead to achieve the aims of that group. So worship leadership exists in order to enable the congregation to worship God. This is a huge responsibility, both spiritually and practically. Most of the book will be looking at the practical issues and these are probably the ones foremost in your mind. But first we are going to explore some of the spiritual issues in daring to lead others in worship.

# 2

# Worshipping God with three eyes: the spirituality of leading others in worship

So leading worship is normally by invitation only. This is not because it is an exclusive club, but because it is a ministry to which we are called by God through the church community.

You may find this invitation scary and so need some encouragement. On the other hand, leading worship may come naturally to you and you may need reminding that it is in fact a great privilege. Above all, we all need to remember that it is a ministry, a service which we undertake for the sake of others. As a result, there are things we give up as a part of that service, sacrifices we make in order to help other people to worship.

Does a worship leader worship? Of course the answer is going to be 'Yes', but are they going to worship in the same way as if they were in a congregation led by someone else? If we were to ponder this question a little more, we would begin to realize that things are not quite as straight-forward as they may first have seemed.

Let's use prayer as an illustration of what I mean. Remind yourself of what you experience when you pray in your own personal devotions. Sometimes you may be able to focus on God such that you become un-aware of your surroundings. Sometimes you might feel like an aeroplane that fails to get off the ground. But occasionally you may experience an intense feeling of longing, or gratitude, or love for God. Now think what it is like to be led in prayer in a church service. The insight, sensitivity and faith of the person leading the prayer might be able to help you focus on God in a way which gives you a deep sense of God's presence and grace.

Now try and imagine what is happening when you are asked to lead the congregation in prayer. Your main responsibility is not primarily to offer your own prayers and be 'lost in wonder, love and praise', but to help other people to pray. Of course, you are still praying, and you need to be sincere in the things you say, but the prayers need to be offered in such a way that the members of the congregation are able to make the prayers their own. One consequence of this is that different congregations may require our praying in different ways. For example, in a family service we will use different language and perhaps follow different themes than in a healing service. If we are leading a small group of friends in a home group we will pray in a different way from when we are leading a congregation of a couple of hundred people. The needs of the situation and the people involved affect how we lead prayer – because our leading prayer is a service to them, as well as to God.

Imagine you are hosting a party where there is a buffet meal. Yes, of course you will have something to eat yourself – and usually at the same time as your guests. But as the host, your first responsibility is to ensure that your guests are fed and have all they need. Only after this will it be time for you to have some food yourself. In a similar way, when you are invited to lead worship you will indeed worship God yourself, but your primary responsibility will be to help others to worship. This means sacrificing the freedom to be lost in what you are doing, and this sacrifice is a large part of your offering to God in that particular service – it is your worship. You will need to worship God in a different way.

## Worshipping God with three eyes

One of the most important differences in how you will worship God when you are leading others in worship is the way in which you pay attention. You can't simply put your head down and worship, or raise your eyes skyward, as though there was just you and God! You are supposed to be leading other people in worship so you need to pay attention to them!

### 1 You need one eye on the congregation

When you are guiding or leading people in an activity you need to keep an eye on them. As well as being clear what it is you are trying to do, you also need to see how they are doing. When we work with other people we constantly make adjustments in the way we work – it's called 'teamwork'. And when we are trying to help others to worship we need to watch their body language to see whether they are engaged or bored, anticipating what will happen next or needing clearer instructions. For example, are some uncertain as to whether they should be standing or sitting? Do you want them to sing something or say a responsive prayer? In addition, there is also the wider sense of a prevailing mood or a variety of feelings which might be part of a congregation on that particular day and which you need to keep an eye on.

You need to lead in such a way that the congregation members are clear about what it is they are being asked to do, while you don't want to labour the point so much that they are more aware of the mechanics of the service rather than worshipping. You want them to be relaxed yet alert – and the best way to achieve that is to watch them and adjust how you lead.

## 2 You need one eye on God

As we shall see later, the worship event is not simply a group of people who come together to remind themselves and to celebrate what they believe. It is a meeting with God as well as a meeting with one another. God is at the centre of our focus, as worshippers and as worship leaders. In part, this will mean that much of what we sing, and all of what we pray, will be directed to God. But it would be mistaken to think of God as a passive receiver of the things we say and do in worship. Through the Holy Spirit, God is at work, prompting and inspiring us in our worship.

Ultimately, we could speak of God as the main worship leader, but we need to be open to God's leading of us as we lead the congregation. Of course, we want God to guide us while we are preparing before a service, not just during the service. But we should also try and be open to God even as we are leading the service. This involves faith and discernment on our part, and it expresses something of the living relationship with God which the worship represents and embodies.

So how might God lead us while we are leading? Some of the things we will say in the service may be unscripted: this will vary from person to person, as some of us have personalities which are more easily able to cope with speaking spontaneously, while others need to have most things we are going to say written down. Of course, the amount we need written down might become less as we become more experienced in leading worship. But sometimes we might have a sense that we need to add something to what we have prepared to say, or change something from what we have written in advance. It may be how we introduce a song, or it may be the words of a prayer. Or we may feel prompted to pray for someone or something that we hadn't anticipated in preparation but which seems 'right' once we are in the service.

All this is very intuitive, and not very easy to explain, but it will become easier and clearer as you become more practised in leading. What is important as you begin is that you have an expectation that God will lead you, whether

> **Exercise**
>
> Try and jot down a few examples of when you have felt prompted to do something unplanned, or when you have noticed that others leading worship have been so prompted.
>
> Can you add to your list some examples of spontaneous changes, which, on further reflection, were not actually very helpful?

through what you have already prepared or through the worship event itself. This is where prayerful preparation is very important. During the service, you need to multi-task and be aware of all sorts of things, but before you lead, and as you prepare, you should be focused on what God wants you to do and how God wants you to lead this congregation. Which takes us to the third, anatomically improbable, eye.

## 3 You need one eye on the clock

Now, by 'the clock' I don't just mean the clock – or the time. An 'eye on the clock' is my way of representing all those very practical things which you need to bear in mind while you are leading worship. Time is important. If you are leading a congregation in worship then you need to take account of the local culture. In some parts of the world it is quite normal for a service to last three hours, but if you work to that timetable in some British congregations then people will either walk out or fall asleep! You need to take account of what people are used to if you are to maintain the congregation's attention,

> **Exercise**
>
> If you have led worship recently, take the written order of service that you used. If not, write down in order all that happened at a recent Sunday service. Now go through the order of service and jot down practical things that the worship leader would need to be thinking about.

so an eye on the clock is a very necessary skill. Of course, it is best if the congregation are not aware of this time watching, as you want them to focus on God and what God is saying to them.

There are various other things which that third eye will need to observe.

There may be someone else about to read the Bible or offer a prayer, and you may need to catch their eye to encourage them or prompt them to come forward. You may need to move a microphone ready for someone to give their testimony – and you will certainly need to keep eye contact with the music leader if you have a music group and are singing the sort of songs which are going to be repeated.

---

### Exercise

You have prepared worship for Sunday, choosing upbeat songs which focus on God's goodness. But on the Saturday a young person from the church is involved in an accident and is killed. The news is spreading on Sunday morning as you stand up to lead the service. What do you do?

You are leading worship, and the band is playing a song you know well and love. As you sing, you realise that the words are not up on the screen behind you and most of the congregation are not singing. What do you do?

---

## Driving with due care and attention

If you think that worshipping with three eyes is too difficult, then remind yourself what it is like to drive a car. The law requires that we should drive with 'due care and attention', yet just think of the various things a driver has to pay attention to at the same time.

First, you need to concentrate on the road in front of you, paying attention to traffic lights, road junctions, speed limit signs and other warnings. You need to note when the road bends and steer accordingly, as well as watching out for reckless pedestrians who may walk out in front of your car. This is paying attention.

Second, you need to know your ultimate destination and how to reach it. You need to be aware of the route, perhaps remembering directions someone has given you ('first left, second right, then look out for the Red Lion pub'), or remembering the route from your perusal of a road atlas. You need to observe landmarks and interpret what you see, connecting it to those directions which may or may not have been clear.

Third, you need to undertake all the routine operations of a driver, working the controls of a machine. As well as steering, you need to operate the gears and clutch – and apply the brakes from time to time. All this while looking where you are going and working out the route.

Finally, you may well have a passenger with whom you share a conversation, or you may listen to the car radio. Either way, you do these things in such a way as not to distract you from driving safely.

This multi-tasking requires our minds working on several levels of consciousness at the same time. We are paying attention, but the attention means a combination of clear focused thought processes as well as certain reflex actions of which we are aware, but at a different level of our consciousness.

This picture of driving a car is a good illustration of how, when we are leading others in worship, we cannot afford to focus on just one thing, however intensely and devoutly we wish to do so. There are other times for single-minded devotion but, while we are leading the community in worship, we must sacrifice that option in order to serve both God and the worshippers. I wonder why the apostle Paul didn't include multi-tasking in the gifts of the Spirit?

Don't be put off by this talk of multi-tasking. Time and practice will make things easier. Whenever you do something new you have to concentrate on every part of the task at first. Soon some parts of the task become second nature – like driving a car! Once you are experienced you don't notice the gear changing – but you do watch the road and navigate to your destination. Leading worship will be like that as well.

# Meanings

# 3

# Why worship?

Aim: To understand the purpose of Christian worship and the implications of its meaning for the way it is led.

So what is Christian worship? It may be obvious to you what worship is about, yet often people do not have a clear idea of what they are doing when they 'go to church'. And even if they answer the question with something like, 'to worship God', do they have a clear idea what such a phrase might mean? If you are invited to lead others in Christian worship then it is important that you do have some understanding of the meaning and purpose of the activity you are leading.

There are various dangers if you do not have a clear idea of what you are doing:

- You will not have guiding principles to help you decide on content or methods.
- You are likely simply to copy other worship you have known rather than intentionally plan for a particular service.
- You are likely to be slipping into a traditional role in a group rather than really leading others in worship.

## Defining worship

Some people see definitions as just playing with words, but they can be very helpful in enabling us to understand what we are doing. Trying to express in words the purpose of our actions can help us to clarify our intentions and make our hard work more effective. When we reflect on possible definitions it is often our recognizing their helpful, and also their less helpful, aspects which sheds most

> **Exercise**
>
> Write here your own definition of worship and its purpose:

light on what we are trying to do. Here are some possible definitions of worship and some comments on them.

> Man's chief end is to glorify God and enjoy him for ever.
>
> (Westminster Shorter Catechism)

This was written in the middle of the seventeenth century (hence the exclusive language) and is often quoted as a reason why we worship. According to this, we worship because we were created to worship and to enjoy a relationship of fellowship with God. This is an important truth – that human beings are designed to relate to God – and it helps us understand why worship is important for us. When we worship we should be more truly alive and more completely fulfilling our human destiny than when we are not.

There is, of course, a duty element to worship – we do it because we ought to worship God. Yet the catechism states that our relationship with God should be a matter of enjoyment, a relationship of delight and pleasure. Often worship may not feel like the expression of delight and we may want to reflect on why this is and what we can do to remedy the situation.

There are things we will want to explore later about both the quality of worship and the relationship of worship to the whole of life. For now, we can reflect that this statement is a helpful starting point about why we worship – but it doesn't really define worship – and wasn't originally intended to. It is a statement about the nature of our humanity and our relationship with God. And in that, it is very important.

Here is another definition of worship:

Worship is the dramatic celebration of God in his supreme worth in such a manner that his worthiness becomes the norm and inspiration of human living.

(Ralph P. Martin, *Worship in the Early Church*)

There are a number of positive features in this attempt to describe the importance of worship. Worship is dramatic and it is a celebration. This definition mentions the 'worthiness' of God and, like many writers, Martin refers to the way that the English word 'worship' comes from an Anglo-Saxon word (*weorthscrip*), which implies dignity and respect. A modern use of this meaning is when in civic events we may refer to 'his or her worship the mayor'. This implies that the mayor, as a representative citizen of a town or city, is worthy of respect and honour.

This definition sees the worship event as focused on God and it acknowledges that the process of worshipping leads to our being drawn to the reality we worship. In the process of worshipping, the worshippers become more like the reality they worship. This is why worship can be exciting and why false worship can be so dangerous. One of the consequences of worshipping God is that the characteristics of God which we celebrate – love, hope, forgiveness, for example – become increasingly important for us in our daily living and not simply abstract aspects of God or commodities we receive from God. To worship God for the love lavished upon us in Jesus Christ is to see love as something to which we aspire as followers of Jesus. To give thanks for God's generous provision for our lives is to open ourselves to the possibility of our being generous as well. Can you see that the things we celebrate about God in worship become very important in how they affect the worshippers? To say false things about God can be very dangerous – not only at the level of orthodox or heretical beliefs, but at the level of how the worshippers are encouraged to behave. So, for example, worshipping a God of vengeance could lead to the worshippers prizing a vengeful attitude to people who cross them.

But there are weaknesses in Martin's definition. It is possible to celebrate how wonderful God is without actually addressing God. Yet worship should have something of the character of an encounter where we engage with God, offering, for example, adoration and dedication, and also receiving from God guidance and forgiveness.

A writer who avoids actually producing a definition but who offers us a number of pictures, of worship, is Susan White. She presents worship as:

- a service to God
- a mirror of heaven
- affirmation
- communion
- proclamation
- the arena of transcendence.

Each of these ideas could be explored separately in detail, but together they highlight the multidimensional nature of the worship event. Here are six different ways in which we could look at worship, and they are not exclusive, but together build up a picture which offers important insights.

Here is my own attempt at a concise definition which describes the nature of the worship event and something of its purpose:

> Christian worship is a gathering of the church, in the name of Jesus Christ and in the power of the Holy Spirit, in order to meet God through Scripture, prayer, proclamation and sacraments, and to seek God's Kingdom.

Let's unpack this:

1  Worship is a gathering of the church, a community of those who have accepted Jesus Christ as Lord and Saviour and who seek to follow him. While we can legitimately talk about someone worshipping God in their personal devotions, when we talk about 'Christian worship' we are normally referring to this communal activity of corporate worship.

2  Worship is not simply a human activity, but an encounter in which the Spirit enables us to meet with God in prayer and through other means. God inspires us to offer worship and helps us in that worship. Look at Romans 8.26–27, where Paul writes about the way God helps us to pray.

3  This communal worship also uses regularly a number of God-given resources. We read the Bible, and in the sermon the preacher applies it to the situation of the congregation; we offer prayer and we gather around the Lord's Table; we sing hymns and someone may encourage others with a testimony of how God has worked in their life.

4  Worship is also a place where we align our will with God's will, for if we place God at the centre of our concerns, what God wants will become what we want – and that means praying for, and seeking, the kingdom of God.

Can you see now how the way we think about worship can affect positively or negatively the way we plan for it and lead it? For example, if our understanding of worship were simply, 'an event in which we praise God and ask for his blessing on our lives', then our worship practice would be significantly different from the worship which might flow from the definitions we have examined.

Here's one final quotation which isn't so much a definition of communal worship as a statement of how true worship results in a profound effect on the worshippers:

> Worship is the submission of all our nature to God. It is the quickening of conscience by His holiness; the nourishment of the mind with His truth; the purifying of imagination by His beauty; the opening of the heart to His love; the surrender of the will to His purpose – and all this is gathered up in adoration, the most selfless attitude of which our nature is capable, and therefore the chief remedy for that self-centredness which is original sin, and the source of all actual sin.
>
> (William Temple, *Readings in St John's Gospel*)

When genuine worship takes place, whether religious or otherwise, the worshipper becomes more like the one worshipped. In hero worship, the admirer tries to emulate the hero and is inspired by that hero's actions, values and preferences. When we worship God, then aspects of the character of God – for example, love, mercy, justice, peace – influence our character and values. If we delight in the gracious and selfless love of God, then we become more loving, or at least have kindled within us a desire to be more loving.

## Purpose and practice

Let's now look at how some of these themes will influence the way we lead worship. In evangelical and free church worship, there may be local or denominational expectations about how a service will unfold (such as the shape and style of a service, which we shall look at later), but there is still a great deal of freedom. This means that while this book can give you guidance for your planning and leading, no authority can require you to follow a particular formula in detail. This freedom can be both exciting and intimidating at the same time. Practical tips and suggestions will come later, but here, having looked at some definitions, we can list some general guidelines which can help you in your overall planning.

1. Christian worship should focus on God, Father, Son and Holy Spirit and be true to what has been shown us in Jesus and recorded for us in Scripture.

2. Christian worship should be planned by the leader and prepared for by the worshippers in such a way as to assume the presence of God and the desire of the worshippers to be open to God.

---

### Exercise

This chapter explores the ideas that worship is an encounter with God, through which we are changed.

In the last chapter I suggested you take an order of service which you have used or write one from a recent service. Take this again and look through it. What parts of this service may have helped the congregation to encounter God, and delight in God's presence and love? What parts might have helped the congregation to be changed by God? Were there parts which actually hindered the congregation from really focusing on God?

What changes or additions might you make to this service so that there could be an even stronger sense of encounter and change? How might, for example, our concern for God's rule in the world and God's kingdom, be expressed and shaped in this worship service?

---

# 4

# Who is worship for?

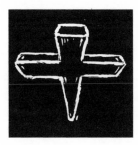

Aim: To explore who worship should be aimed at and whose concerns should be at the forefront of the worship leader's mind.

So who is worship for? This is a useful question to ask. We live in a consumer society where most people are used to making decisions about what products to buy, and so get into an attitude of mind which is very choosy. If you don't like one shop, then you go to another. The trouble is that many people have this attitude about church, and this can lead to a sense that the church has to provide worship which will satisfy prospective customers – oops, sorry – worshippers.

Anyone leading worship needs to tackle the question of whom they are serving. Is the most important thing to keep the regular congregation happy? Or should we be designing worship which will attract newcomers and draw them towards Christian believing? Or should we have a 'take-it-or-leave-it' approach which is based on what we believe God wants from our worship and not what the congregation might want?

So who is worship for? Well, there is more than one answer to this.

## 1 Worship is for God

By definition, worship is focused on a reality which/who is being worshipped. Praise and thanksgiving are directed to God and, ultimately, we must say that our worship is for God. An important aspect of genuine worship is the act of offering – and not just the collection of money. Our offering in worship can include the offering of our praise and thanksgiving, the offering, or dedicating, of our lives for God's service, and even the offering of our confession – the acknowledgment of our sins, as well as our repentance and our abandonment to God's grace and mercy. We give these to God, so, in a real sense, the worship of the congregation is for God.

Worship leaders must offer their planning to God and ask for help so that all they do in the leading of worship is a worthy offering to the One who has made and redeemed us. This means that preparation will include prayer as well as careful planning. Offering their best to God should include, on the one hand, thorough practical preparation and, on the other hand, the preparation of their hearts through prayer and the opening of themselves to God's guidance through the work of the Holy Spirit.

Some people, however, have tried to say that this is all we can say – that worship is for God and that to plan worship as though it was for the benefit of the congregation is to misuse the worship event. But it is part of God's gracious plan that, when we truly worship God, there are beneficial consequences for the worshippers in addition to God being praised. So:

## 2 Worship is for the church community

When we truly worship God, the church community is built up and encouraged. In one sense, we could say that this is a by-product of worship but, because the church exists to be a community in relationship with God, good worship should lead to an enriching and strengthening of the church.

Remember that not all the words in a service are addressed to God. Many, like the readings and the sermon, are addressed to the congregation, both collectively and to its individual members. We have already thought about worship as an encounter between God and the congregation. It can be helpful to look at what is said in worship as a dialogue in which the congregation brings prayers to God, and then, through Scripture and preaching, God addresses the congregation which, in turn, responds in prayer and dedication.

When we look at the shape of worship services, we will see that this basic pattern is usually nuanced by additional back and forth movements: often an opening call to worship will represent God inviting the congregation to worship, and the final dismissal and blessing will represent God sending the congregation out into the world in witness and service.

The church gathers week by week to worship God. This community places itself under the authority of the rule of Christ and comes ready to listen to God's word and to obey his commands. This weekly paying attention to God, as well as the activities of praising and confessing, of thanking and dedication, shape this worshipping community into a Christian community which reflects the God it worships and the Christ it aspires to follow.

However, at this point we need to note a health warning. The quality of worship (and we will return later to what that might mean) can affect the health of the congregation, so it is important to think about the needs of the congregation when planning worship. Worship which expresses the Christian truth of God will be likely to influence congregations in a positive way. However, when God is misrepresented in what we say, or the way we do things, then this can have negative effects on the worshippers.

Additionally, we may present good orthodox teaching about God, but if we don't take account of the needs of worshippers (and perhaps we might bore them and they no longer pay attention) then the worship may not build up the church at all.

## 3 Worship is for the worshippers

If you ask a regular worshipper why they attend worship (and that word 'attend' begs all sorts of questions) they might say that it is in order to worship God. In addition, or even instead, they may say something like 'It helps me to cope with the rest of the week', or 'It encourages and strengthens me in my living the Christian life', or 'It gives me comfort and I like the fellowship'. Each of these can have some validity.

Individual worshippers have their own needs and, by the grace of God, some of these may be met when we come and offer God our worship. Taking those needs, so far as you know them, into account when planning worship need not mean giving in to consumerism. Remember that these people were created to share fellowship with God – but God created them in great variety, and many knocks and opportunities in life have added further to that variety.

There is something very specific about leading worship. You are called to lead this community of persons in this place on this day in the worship of God. Worship should be contextual, sensitive to the particularities of the people and the situation. One of the challenges of leading worship is therefore to know something about the needs of that particular congregation, whether it is your usual place of worship, or a church you are visiting, and to think about how you might set about discovering those needs. As we shall see, people can be shaped in their discipleship, formed in their faith, challenged and encouraged in good worship. But the converse is also true: poor worship can lead to questionable views of God, or dysfunctional relationships, and can depress people or make them dependent. We have to take these things seriously when we are entrusted with leading worship.

Of course, worshippers and worship leaders can fall prey to the spirit of consumerism. If the most important concern of the worship leader is achieving 'satisfied customers', or if the overriding concern of the worshipper is having worship 'the way I like it', then something is wrong. This is why we need to be very clear about the purpose of worship, as well as its influence for good or ill on the members of the congregation.

## 4 Worship is for the world

If worship is partly concerned with seeking God's kingdom, then worshippers will pray for the needs of the world and be encouraged to serve God by serving their neighbours in a variety of ways. In true worship we bring the world to God and are sent back into the world commissioned and blessed.

We shall consider later the ways in which worship leaders can enable connections to be made between the wider world and what happens in the worship service. For now, we must remind ourselves that worship must never become a cosy place where we 'escape' from the problems and joys of the world. God is the God of creation and this God 'so loved the world that he sent his only Son'. One form of words that is sometimes used to end a service makes this very point: 'The worship is over. Let the service begin.'

It is true that in worship we will want to focus on God and this will mean trying to avoid distractions. Yet the God on whom we focus is the One who is passionately concerned about the world, and our worship must reflect that reality. Any worship which avoids the needs of the world for which Christ died is not going to be worship which is true to the gospel – now there's a thought!

## Exercise

In previous chapters we have been working with an 'order of service' that you have put together or written down. Find that again, and if possible two or three other 'orders of service'. This chapter looks at four different answers to the question, 'Who is worship for?' Look through the orders of service and try and identify which individual parts (a song, a prayer, the offering, the notices, etc.) connect to these four different answers. Write alongside each of these parts one of these four headings: God, Congregation, Individual, World. Looking at this list, did the service have the right kind of balance? Did the balance change between the different services?

# 5

# Worship and life: a continuing journey

Aim: To explore the ways in which our worship of God is connected to the living of our daily lives.

As we have looked at the meaning of worship – what we are trying to do and who worship is really for – we have seen that worship is about meeting God. The heart of worship is an encounter in which we seek God's presence, offer prayers and make ourselves available to receive God's word and blessing. We have seen that this meeting with God cannot be taken for granted, but it is what worship is about!

But before we look in more detail at the different parts of a worship service, we need to explore another aspect of what worship is and what it means. We need to examine the relationship of worship to the rest of life.

## Worship as escape

'Lord, help us to forget the worries and concerns of our daily lives and focus on you.' Have you ever prayed a prayer like that, or heard someone else pray it? We talk about 'entering God's presence' and 'being taken out of ourselves for a while' but, while this may seem quite a natural way of understanding worship, there is something deeply disturbing about it.

Yes, worship is encounter with God and, yes, we do want to pay God full attention and, no, we don't want to be thinking of the Sunday dinner or the afternoon football on TV. But there is something very dysfunctional about worship which tries to evade the world in which we are called to follow Jesus Christ, however much we package it as a passionate concern to love God and revel in God's presence.

God is not a cuddly teddy bear or a comfort blanket, and while Scripture speaks of God as a 'refuge', this image suggests a place of security amidst the troubles that assail us – not a place of avoidance or escape. The God we worship is intimately concerned with the world which is God's own creation, and to seek God is not the same as to escape from the world.

In fact, we cannot escape the world – we bring it to worship with us, within our own hearts. When we confess our sins and when we praise God for creation we are taking the world, and our part in it, seriously. When we remember Jesus Christ, and give thanks for all God has done and given through him, we are celebrating a God who takes the world so seriously that he becomes a part of it through the incarnation.

Worship should not be apart from life, but should be a part of life. Real, authentic, 'truly spiritual' worship will have a strong connection with the rest of our existence. It will celebrate life, it will seek God's justice and healing and will constantly pay attention to the God who 'so loved the world that he gave his only son'. So how can we talk about this connectedness, the relationship between worship and the whole of life?

## Worship as focus

Because we normally meet with others in a special place, usually a church building, to worship God, it is easy to think of worship and life as though they were in two separate compartments of our lives. Indeed some people refer to the place where we worship as a 'sanctuary', as though we were indeed running away from life to a place of safety!

And there will be things we will do in worship, or arrangements we will make, the purpose of which will be to help us to pay attention to God. So the place of worship may have a visual focus – an altar, or a cross, or even a screen with images – designed to help us to concentrate on God and God's love for us. In addition, much of the music which will be played, or the songs we will be encouraged to sing, will aim at helping us to pay attention to God.

This idea of 'paying attention' is important because, especially in western society, we are encouraged to be spectators. We watch events on television, while chatting to family or eating our tea and we are removed from the action. Much would be gained in our relationships if we learned to 'pay attention' more to each other. Worship, also, can be helped by our paying attention and not being half-interested, multi-tasking spectators.

Yet this paying attention is not to the exclusion of everything else – because God is concerned about everything else. So how can we visualize this paying attention which isn't escapism? The image which I think can help us is that of 'focus'. When you look through the right kind of lens it brings what is in front of you into sharper focus. (Of course, if you look through the wrong  kind of lens, or the wrong way through a lens, then things become more distant or more blurred!)

Perhaps you have tried that experiment where you take a magnifying glass and focus the sun's rays on a piece of paper or some dry grass. The warmth of the sun which you can feel on your skin is magnified to such a heat that the paper or the grass catch fire. The lens gathers and intensifies the rays which are already present. In worship we focus on God – but in such a way that God and God's world are brought into sharper focus. That which is true all the time becomes clearer and more focused through our worship. We talk about 'entering God's presence' but God is always with us in the world – it's just that in worship we make ourselves more aware of that presence.

In worship we see things more clearly than at other times. We see that the fundamental reality of the universe is God's love. We see that the world is not there for our plundering, but is God's creation with which we are entrusted. We see that human relationships are not inevitably blighted by hurt and retribution, but can be transformed by love and forgiveness. We see God, and everything else is seen differently.

## Worship as practice and rehearsal

But worship is not only about seeing things differently, though that is a necessary beginning. It is also about making a difference to the world when we leave the worship event. So we can also see worship as a preparation for living – a time when we practise living in a Christian way and when we rehearse the attitudes, insights and intentions which will be an important part of living for God in God's world.

We pay attention to God and we listen to God's word and ask God's help in connecting it to our lives. But in worship we do more because we begin to practise what is preached and we start to rehearse the kind of relationships and attitudes which God wants for us. This is part of what I meant earlier when I spoke about 'seeking God's kingdom'.

So when we give thanks to God in worship, we are not only thanking him for this or that, we are learning to view the world with gratitude and to see and experience life as a gift. When we pray for the world, we are also forming certain attitudes in ourselves, feeling for the world as we believe God feels for the world, and that will make a difference to our actions. When we share the peace in worship we are practising being a community founded on forgiveness, healed by reconciliation. This isn't escape from the world, but engagement with it through the grace of God.

Worship is a kind of laboratory or classroom where conditions are protected and controlled. Here we can experiment in forgiving and giving thanks, here we can hear the gospel and apply it to our lives. When we leave worship we leave the protected and controlled environment and field test the things we have learned. In worship, it is as though we learn to swim in a swimming pool, and when we leave we have to learn to swim in the sea. The swimming pool is a necessary first stage of learning and prepares us for the ocean. Once we have been buffeted by waves and coped with a heavy swell, we may want to return to the pool to develop our technique. So in worship we return to re-learn what has been buffeted by the world.

Worship and life are connected. If we try and separate them we will come unstuck. Our living will lose its Christian identity and our worship will lose its Christian integrity. To try and focus on God as a way of getting away from the problems of everyday life is to go searching after a false god. To focus on the Christian God is to encounter the God whose will is that the earth should be transfigured, and broken human beings be made whole.

## Worship as dedication

There is another way in which we can understand the connection between worship and the whole of life. Worship, as we mentioned in the previous chapter, is about the giving of ourselves to God – the offering of

31

our love, our praise, our realism about ourselves; the offering of our time and talents and money, and, ultimately, the offering of our willingness to follow Jesus. In other words, this offering of ourselves to God isn't the dedication of some kind of disembodied self, it is the offering of who we are – our social selves, our lives at work and play and in relationship, it is the offering of our lives in the world, not just some spiritual self at worship 'in church'.

The apostle Paul wrote to the Romans, imploring them to give their whole lives to God. He used the image of a temple sacrifice as he invited them to give all the dimensions of their lives to God:

> I appeal to you therefore, brothers and sisters, by the mercies of God, to present your bodies as a living sacrifice, holy and acceptable to God, which is your spiritual worship. Do not be conformed to this world, but be transformed by the renewing of your minds, so that you may discern what is the will of God – what is good and acceptable and perfect.
>
> (Romans 12.1–2)

In the rest of the chapter he spells out what this offering means. It means the way we treat one another as Christians, it means how we react to persecution or adversity; it is about love, hope and perseverance in prayer. So we offer the whole of life to God, and that most intense of prayers in worship, the prayer when we give ourselves to God, is the time when most completely worship and life, God's purposes and our wills, coincide.

## Beginnings and endings

If worship is going to be connected with the whole of life, then the beginning and the end of the service will be key moments of connection, joining this moment of worship with the rest of life. The join may be expressed at the beginning by a welcome and a call to worship, such as a sentence of Scripture which reminds us about God or some aspect of the good news of Jesus Christ. At the end of the service the join with life may be effected through a commission to go out in the name of Christ and the words of a blessing and assurance that God goes with us.

Another way of seeing these joins is to talk about the service beginning with the gathering of the congregation and ending with its being sent out into the world. We will look more closely at this in the next chapter, but we gather around the word of God which is the main means by which

God makes himself known to us today. Through Scripture we learn of Jesus Christ, his ministry and mission, cross and resurrection. Through Scripture, we learn of God's promises and faithfulness before Christ and the coming of the Holy Spirit to transform and bring new life to the world and our lives. The spiral diagram (see page 34) is helpful because it both describes this gathering, or centring, around God in Scripture, and expresses the forward momentum of the worship event which moves from opening worship, through praise and prayer, listening and responding, to the sending out of the congregation in God's name and with God's blessing to do God's work. This forward momentum is important and in the next chapter we shall begin to look at how planning the various parts of the service can move the congregation forward, on a journey which focuses on God and then goes in God's name into God's world.

So you have been invited to lead worship. Perhaps now you can see that this doesn't primarily mean leading the congregation in a series of static worship moments, but leading them on a journey towards God and then towards God's world. This is an awesome responsibility – but it is also an exciting opportunity to serve and to discover that God is good.

---

### Exercise

Try writing a worship journal, for a few weeks or months. Journals are a long-established way of helping individuals to focus on God. Soon after each service, whether you were involved in leading it or were a participant, write down the ways that the worship made connections with the rest of your life, perhaps helping to focus on something important at the moment, or enabling you to offer something to God. This journal will not only enable you to look back on your walk with God, but will give you some insight into the way worship and life interact.

---

# 6

# Shapes and patterns

Aim: To understand how the shape of a service can help a congregation to be actively involved in the worship and to explore the possibilities which various patterns offer.

One of the challenges of leading free church worship is deciding the overall shape of the service. Worship leaders in liturgical traditions will already have a fixed form in their service book – they will simply need to choose Bible readings, hymns and some prayers and fit them into an existing framework. In free church worship, however, there may be a usual sequence of events (often called an 'order of service') but that sequence is not mandatory and there is flexibility about what happens when.

Of course, local custom may be less flexible and it is important to know both the usual order of service and local attitudes to significant changes! Relationships are as important in communal worship as elsewhere.

## Why bother with shapes?

So why bother with the sequence in which things happen in a service? Surely we should be more concerned with the sincerity of the worship leader and the congregation than with the formality of a fixed running order? Shouldn't we be free to do what feels right on the day? What about being open to the guidance of the Holy Spirit? These attitudes are certainly around, so how do we respond to them?

First, remember that worship is a communal activity, something which we do together. Whenever you are leading a group of people in any collective activity you need to lead in such a way that the individual members of the group are able to focus on the same things at the same time and act together. In worship this can be helped in all sorts of ways, and one of the best ways is to have a clear sequence in which things happen, an order which people recognize as being a good way to do whatever you are doing.

Second, if everything is spontaneous it is easy for there to be confusion and misunderstanding. The apostle Paul wrote: 'all things should be done decently and in order' (1 Corinthians 14.40). At times spontaneity will be important, but it is all the more powerful when it happens within a framework where things fit together and make sense – both to the leader and to the congregation.

Third, God has given us minds, and Jesus' summing up of the law includes loving God 'with all your heart, and with all your soul, and with all your mind, and with all your strength' (Mark 12.30). The mind is not the enemy of the heart, but is a gift of God which we use in our worship along with our heart and the whole of ourselves. A shape to worship helps the members of the congregation to understand what they are doing and so to enter more fully into it. Then the mind helps the heart and focuses on the meaning of the worship.

## What kind of shape?

### Exercise

Cut some small pieces of paper (perhaps a sheet of A4 into 8 pieces). On each piece of paper write one thing that you think might happen in a Sunday service.

When you have exhausted your ideas begin to play with these pieces of paper. Choose some and put them in the order, on a table or the floor, in which they might happen. Move some of the pieces of paper around in the order, and put them in what you think are unusual orders; swap some with others you have not yet used.

Each time you make a new shape, think about what it might feel like to be in that service. Do you think it would work well? Why, or why not?

Try to describe the different shapes that you make, and particularly the shapes that you think would work well.

Hopefully you will have seen that there is meaning in the shape of the service, and that some shapes don't work as well as others. It would seem odd, for example, if a service began with a sermon, followed by readings and prayers and hymns and songs. Sometimes specialist writers on worship have talked about 'the deep structures' of worship or 'the dynamic movements' of a service. Quite apart from the links between one item and another, there can often be major sections of a service where the focus is on a particular action – such as praise, or listening to God's word or responding to God. Within these sections various items such as hymns or prayers may be grouped together, helping us to concentrate. The way we move from one section of the service to another can also be significant. Thus the shape of a service can help our attention, our togetherness and our sense of the event of worship 'meaning something' and 'going somewhere'.

As you have rearranged your pieces of paper and experimented with different shapes it may be that you have formed a shape of worship common in your own and other churches. It may also be that you have recognized that those shapes which seem as if they would work well are those that move us on in different ways through the service. We could use two different images to describe this movement.

## Journey and dialogue

The first image is that of a journey. The way we move from one section of the service to another can be like walking through the rooms of a house or passing various landmarks on a familiar journey. Indeed, this idea of journey is very significant. For reasons which will become clear later, I believe that a service should not be a static collection of units, but a dynamic journey in which the congregation is led through a number of actions in which they encounter God and God's word and are then sent out into the world in witness and service. This means that when we look at the basic shapes of worship we shall ask whether they enable such a journey to take place and, if not, how they might be adapted to do so.

> **Exercise**
>
> Look back to the various shapes you made with the pieces of paper. Trace the way that different orders enable both a journey and a dialogue.
>
> Notice the way that different orders will take us on a slightly different journey, or emphasize the dialogue in different ways.

The second image is that of dialogue. Worship, I have suggested, is both for God and the congregation, a time when those who gather encounter God as part of an ongoing relationship. We can expect, therefore, that when we meet together for worship God will speak with us, notably through Scripture and sermon, and we will speak with God, through prayer and singing, but also through other parts of the service, such as the offering. This conversation will continue through the service. This means that when we look at the basic shapes of worship we shall ask whether they enable such a dialogue to take place and, if not, how they might be adapted to do so.

Because most free church services do not include the Lord's Supper, or Holy Communion, we shall concentrate here on 'services of the word' where Scripture takes a pre-eminent place. We shall look at communion shapes in Chapter 15.

While free church worship is theoretically free to take an almost infinite variety of forms, it effectively falls into three basic shapes with many variations and blends between them. You may have made these shapes yourself. We shall introduce them in turn and explore both their opportunities and their drawbacks.

## The hymn sandwich

This is often regarded as the traditional shape of a free church service. In fact, it only dates from the end of the nineteenth century, but was almost universal by the middle of the twentieth century. It is still common in some more traditional churches, and someone who begins to lead worship and preach in churches other than their own may well find this pattern in some of those churches.

There are two features of this shape (shown in Figure 1) which stand out. First, the service is interspersed with congregational singing – hence the nickname 'hymn sandwich'! Second, the sermon is effectively the climax of the service. Here is one way of demonstrating the importance of Scripture, because the preaching

**The hymn sandwich**

- Invitation to worship
- Hymn
- Bible reading
- Hymn
- Prayer
- Notices
- Offering and prayer of dedication
- Hymn
- Sermon
- Hymn
- Benediction

**Figure 1**

should be an exposition of God's word (see Chapter 13) and an application of that word to the local circumstances of the congregation.

One practical advantage of this shape is its simplicity. Through the hymns it also provides regular opportunities for the congregation to stretch their legs (and so aid concentration) and, more importantly, offers a number of opportunities for the congregation outwardly to contribute to the service.

However, there are a number of major weaknesses with the hymn sandwich because this form struggles to express both a sense of journey and a sense of dialogue. First, there is no obvious logic to the sequence of units other than the sermon coming near the end as a climax. This can have the effect of devaluing the rest of worship, both by the arbitrary links between the units, and by the sense that they are preliminaries to the main act – the sermon. Second, the service is quite static and there is little sense of progression, other than preparing for the sermon. Finally, unless there is some adaptation, the only opportunity of responding to the preached word is the hymn which follows the sermon. There appears to be little scope for dynamic movement or much place for responding to what God might say or do during the worship.

Nonetheless, this will be the starting point for leading worship in some churches; it is possible to 'tweak' the shape in such a way that there is some sense of movement and some logic to the sequence of the parts of the service.

### Modified hymn sandwich

- Notices and greeting
- Invitation to worship
- Hymn of praise
- Prayer of adoration and confession
- Hymn of thanksgiving
- Offering and prayer of dedication
- Prayer of intercession
- Bible readings
- Hymn of trust
- Sermon
- Prayer of response
- Hymn enabling response
- Benediction

**Figure 2**

Figure 2 shows a modified form of the hymn sandwich as an illustration of how this tweaking can transform the shape without making huge changes which might alienate a traditional congregation. The readings have been brought nearer the sermon, so as to strengthen the sense that the sermon grows out of the reading of God's word, and a prayer is planned to enable the worship leader or preacher to help the congregation make an appropriate response to the sermon. This may be a prayer of personal dedication, a prayer of thanksgiving or even a prayer of penitence – depending on what the main thrust of the sermon has been. In addition, by ensuring a specific focus for each hymn, it is possible for the congregational singing to be an integral part of the movement from praise to openness to God and a response which leads back into the world. As you continue to play with those pieces of paper you might modify the traditional hymn sandwich in other ways that allow the progression and sense of dialogue to come out.

Another, increasingly common, way in which this shape might be modified is by expanding the first (or indeed any) hymn into a sequence of hymns and songs. This not only increases the congregation's active participation in the service, it opens up the possibility of more movement – provided the songs are chosen carefully. You can see an example of this in Figure 3.

| **Modified hymn sandwich with songs** |
| --- |
| • Notices and greeting |
| • Invitation to worship |
| • Song |
| • Scripture verse |
| • Song |
| • Short prayer |
| • Song |
| • Prayer |
| • Hymn of thanksgiving |
| • Offering and prayer of dedication |
| • Prayer of intercession |
| • Bible readings |
| • Hymn of trust |
| • Sermon |
| • Prayer of response |
| • Song |
| • Short prayer |
| • Song |
| • Benediction |
| **Figure 3** |

## Word and response

This shape has become common in more formal congregations, though as a shape it is open to a variety of worship styles. The basic idea is one of encounter or conversation between God and humanity.

The logic of this shape is that our worship is a meeting with God. We begin by focusing on God in praise and confession. We then read God's word, and its meaning is explored and applied in the sermon. The service then moves to a period of response in which we face God, the world and ourselves differently in the light of God's word. We re-dedicate ourselves to God's service, we pray for God's world and we bring our gifts for God to use in Church and community. Finally, we are commissioned to leave worship and re-enter the everyday world as witnesses to the gospel and

## Service of Word and Response

Our Approach to God

- Notices and greeting
- Call to worship
- Hymn of praise
- Prayer of adoration and confession

God's Word

- Bible readings
- Hymn of thanksgiving
- Sermon

Our Response

- Hymn enabling response
- Prayer of intercession
- Offering and prayer of dedication
- Hymn of trust
- Dismissal and Blessing

**Figure 4**

we are reminded of God's gracious promise to be with us always and everywhere.

This shape can be represented by a diagram using a number of arrows to suggest movement, as in Figure 4. At the beginning of the service the congregation gathers to worship God. So the arrows converge as people gather – but they also turn upwards to remind us that the gathering is more than simply a social event – we gather to meet God; and as we meet God we offer praise and acknowledge our own sinfulness.

Then we listen to God's word being read and expounded. A simple representation of this might be one arrow pointing downwards to indicate God's word coming to us. We also are doing something here – bringing our attentiveness and listening with open hearts to God's word and the promptings of the Holy Spirit. The dominant symbol at this stage, however, is of God speaking to us, so the downward arrow is printed in bold.

The third part of the service is primarily our response to what God has said to us through Scripture and preacher. Here the upward arrow is in bold to represent the dedication of our lives, together with the offering of prayer and our gifts. But still there is a downward arrow because what we offer to God is only made possible by God's grace and the work of the Spirit within us.

Finally, our response includes our readiness to re-enter God's world, commissioned for service and empowered with God's promises and blessing. This is something we do, but we are commissioned, empowered and blessed by the God who goes with us – so the bold arrows represent both our going out in service and witness and God accompanying us in blessing and grace.

The arrows offer a symbolic snapshot of each part of the service, but we can also see in this pattern the shape of a journey with these arrows representing stages on that route from being gathered for worship to being sent out in mission. Things don't have to happen in this sequence, but there is a logic to the order in which things happen that can be helpful. Even if you use a different shape, these four stages are important and can act as a checklist for you when you design a service. For a balanced diet of worship all these stages should be present, whatever the sequence in which you arrange them.

## The three-decker worship event

The other main shape of worship services in the free churches is in three parts, rather like the acts of a play (see Figure 5). It is usually found in churches which would describe themselves as 'evangelical' or 'charismatic', although the shape is no guarantee that the church will be either! The historical origins are in nineteenth century revivalism, but its most common expression today is within charismatic churches, or those who have been influenced in their worship by the charismatic movement. Sometimes people will talk about a 'praise and worship' style of service, or 'contemporary'

---

**Three-decker worship**

- 'Worship time' — Usually as a sequence of songs, with prayers.

- Sermon — Usually, but not always preceded by Scripture reading.

- Ministry time — Prayers for healing and help (often for individuals who come forward), an active response to the sermon and the exercising of charismata or spiritual gifts. The offering of faith in response to the proclamation of the gospel.

**Figure 5**

worship and, while this will usually refer to the kind of music which is used, the service will often be shaped in this three-part pattern.

This pattern begins with an extended period of praise in which God is honoured and in which the worshippers express their devotion and love. Often God will be asked to inspire the worshippers by the moving of the Holy Spirit and the emphasis will be on an encounter between God and the worshippers, in which the good news of the gospel is celebrated, the faith of the worshippers is increased and God is glorified through sincere devotion and adoration.

This part will mainly comprise a series of songs and hymns which may be linked by short prayers, Scripture sentences and simple instructions from the worship leader inviting the members of the congregation to be both intense and honest in their devotion to God.

The sermon brings a significant change of mood and may be quite informal in style. The content of the sermon will depend on the type of church or Christian group in which the worship is taking place, but should, as with all preaching, be based on Scripture. Usually it will involve some kind of challenge, and the final section of the service may well offer an opportunity to respond to its particular challenges.

The third part will vary, but its key element will indicate a belief that we need to respond to God in some way and that God, through the Holy Spirit, will help us in this. So, in a charismatic service this may involve an open time of worship in which people offer spontaneous prayers or words of prophecy, as well as speaking or singing in tongues or offering prayer for the healing of individuals in the congregation. On evangelistic occasions this third part may include an appeal for people to respond in penitence and faith to the gospel and they may be invited to come to the front of the church as an expression of this. Again, the focus is on our doing something with God's help.

---

**Exercise**

Look once more at your pieces of paper. We have thought about shape, but also just begun to think about content. What pieces of paper, and so individual elements, do you think should *always* be in a service and which might be included *sometimes*?

---

This is a very popular form of service, though often this popularity stems from the style of music employed. As a shape, the three-part pattern emphasizes worship as an encounter with God and reminds us that God seeks to move and influence us in that encounter.

However, it can have its weaknesses. The three parts can be disconnected and there may be little flow through the service as a whole. The opening worship may be disjointed, though, when the song material is carefully chosen and sensitively linked, it can take people on a journey which enables them to worship God in a profound way. Sometimes this opening section is referred to as 'a time of worship', as though the rest of the service were not worship. This is a mistake, as is the danger of narrowing down our understanding of 'worship' simply to praise and devotion.

## Going for gold

There is much more that can be said about worship patterns, but these three basic shapes represent three main ways of organizing the worship service, particularly in free churches. They remind us that there is no one perfect order of service and that each has opportunities and pitfalls. So how can we ensure that, whichever shape we use, we will prepare and lead healthy Christian worship? Here are two suggestions which you can apply to any shape with the aim of doing the best you can.

### 1 Use the full range of resources and moods

Variety is the spice of life – in fact, life is varied and so worship should take account of all the possible strands which make up our lives. We should offer praise and confess our sins, we should pray for ourselves and for the needs of the world, we should offer our devotion and struggle to understand the deep mysteries of our faith, we should come in simple faith and pray fervently for more justice in God's world. All these may not figure in every service, but they should all have a place over a period of time.

Similarly, our worship should use a variety of resources. A service may have a dominant culture – whether it's traditional organ music or Christian rock – but we should always be trying to enrich the worship with a breadth of cultural forms. Look for opportunities to include drama, or music in a style different from the main one of the service; use material from the world church and look for ways of taking the congregation a bit further than it expects to go.

### 2 Stepping stones for a journey

Each of these shapes will suffer if the worship is static or bitty and doesn't flow. Many people find the picture of a journey a helpful metaphor which

can organise the service in creative and pastorally responsive ways. This can give movement to each of the shapes or, indeed, help you to create a new shape.

We can visualise this idea of a journey by the simple illustration of a spiralling arrow (see page 34). The congregation gathers for worship and in the course of that worship focuses on God through singing, prayer and Scripture. It gathers around the word of God in order to be addressed by God who then sends the worshippers back into the world. The progress of the journey is enabled through the various units which make up the service – the hymns and songs, the prayers and actions such as the offering and the blessing. These are the stepping stones which enable the congregation to come close enough to God to offer praise and to listen to God's word. They can also be the stepping stones which enable the congregation to return to God's world, commissioned and equipped for service. What a journey this can be – and what a privilege and a challenge to be entrusted with leading the people of God in this journey of worship!

### Exercise

Choose one of the following themes and then plan a service in each of the three main shapes in turn. Experiment with different elements you might include and in different orders. What did you discover about the opportunities of each pattern?

Possible themes for a service: *hope, God's mercy, forgiveness, creation, or peace.*

# Journeying

# 7

# Planning the journey

> Aim: To learn how to design creative and flexible worship events.

A worship service or 'event' shouldn't be a shapeless collection of miscellaneous items. It should have pattern and purpose – it should have forward momentum and direction. In the previous section we looked at a number of patterns which are common in different free churches and tried to see how they might be 'tweaked' or modified. In this chapter we will attempt to get behind the various patterns which have developed over time and to get back to the movement and stages within worship on which they are based. Our aim is to explore how worship leaders can enable the congregation to go on a journey where it meets God and is commissioned for continuing service in the world.

## Plotting and guiding the journey

A key picture which we used in the previous chapter was that of the worship event as a journey. The kind of journey we are after, however, is not an aimless ramble but an intentional progression which visits the right places and ends up by sending the worshippers out in the right direction! We

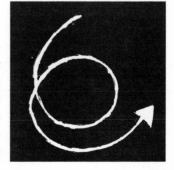

have seen the basic symbol of a spiral as a good way of illustrating this. It is important to note that the symbol includes an arrow because the whole spiral then suggests movement – it begins with gathering for worship, it continues meeting God through Scripture and it moves towards and beyond the commissioning of the congregation to go out in service and witness.

What is most important in this image is the sense of forward momentum. The worship leader has a major responsibility in ensuring both that this movement happens and happens in such a way that it visits the right places on the way. This will be achieved both in the planning stage – as the journey is plotted – and in the actual leading of the service – as the journey is guided.

By 'the right places' I mean that the journey should include such things as praise and confession, thanksgiving and dedication. The focus should always be on God and God's goodness, love and grace. Plotting the journey means preparing and planning the service in such a way that the congregation 'touches enough bases'. Often, or even usually, a service should have an over-arching theme, one which is located in the Bible reading, one which the preacher expounds and which prayers and songs explore. But even so, it is important that certain basic things happen in a service. Whatever, the theme, God should be praised and thanked, and the members of the congregation should have the opportunity to confess their sins and ask for God's help. Worship needs to be a journey in which certain places need to be visited.

The importance of the journey image is that it helps us to see worship as an 'event-in-time', something which has a beginning, a middle and an end – an idea we shall explore in more detail in the chapters on preaching. For now, we can simply state the obvious: worship happens – that's why I tend to call it a worship 'event' – something which happens in real time. Now time is a one-way street – you can't jump around or go back, you have to go forward as the clock continues ticking. Perhaps when worship leaders and preachers forget the clock the worshippers reach for their watches! When you plan an event you think about the sequence of events, the order in which they happen and what transitions and links will take you from one moment to the next. Seeing worship as an event, or a journey through time, encourages us to think about how we are going to plan that journey, which stepping stones we are going to use, what boundaries we are going to cross – and how we are going to help all the group make the journey.

## Moving forward

Let's use another image which can help us. Think of a stage play. If you read the script you can look at the end first, skim from scene to scene and generally be in control of what you read and when you read it. When you are part of a theatre audience you have no such control. You watch the play as the drama unfolds as it has been written by the author or planned by the director. You are in a one-way street, travelling at a speed and direction decided by others. If you misunderstand a scene, or cannot hear clearly a piece of dialogue, there is nothing you can do other than try to pick up the thread of the story which continues relentlessly to its, hopefully, dramatic conclusion.

Such a play is not intended primarily to be a written art form (though many school children may experience the plays of Shakespeare that way). It is intended to be a 'live' art form which, as well as being dramatic and visual, is oral and aural, that is, spoken and heard – not written and read! Similarly, worship is a living event, and the members of the congregation need to be helped to move together through its actions and moments.

Returning to the image of a journey, we could for a moment think about a very short journey – through the rooms of a building. We travel from room to room and in each room participate in whatever activity that room usually accommodates. So we may relax in the lounge, cook and wash up in the kitchen, eat in the dining room and sleep in the bedroom. Yet as we move from room to room there comes a point where we pass through a doorway, when we cross a threshold. One moment we are in the lounge and the next we are in the dining room, and, in between, we have crossed a threshold.

We could think of visiting various rooms in worship, where we praise God or listen to Scripture, where we respond to God's word or prepare to leave. The worship leader needs to guide the congregation through the appropriate doorways, crossing thresholds from praise to confession, from listening to responding.

Let's now mix our metaphors! We could think of the acts of a play and the rooms of the house as the main sections (or stages!) of a worship event. In a play, the order in which the acts are performed is very important. Similarly, in worship the main sections should have a sense of following one another in a logical way. That is not to say that the order should always be the same, though it usually will. For example, praise will usually (though not necessarily always) come near the beginning, and our response to God's word logically has to come after we have heard that word. But it is the principle of planning which is most important – not that there is only one sequence, but that there should be a thought-out sequence, whatever it might be.

Within each main section there will usually be smaller items which, in turn, will need to be arranged in a way that naturally leads from one to the next and so on, rather like the scenes of a play. Some specialists who have written about worship have taken an idea from the social sciences and have distinguished between what they call the 'deep structures' of the worship event and the 'surface structures' of that event. We could see the deep structures as the acts of the play, or the stages of a journey, and the surface structures as the dialogues and actions within the play, or steps on the journey. This could help us, for example, to map the journey of a worship event like that shown in Figure 1.

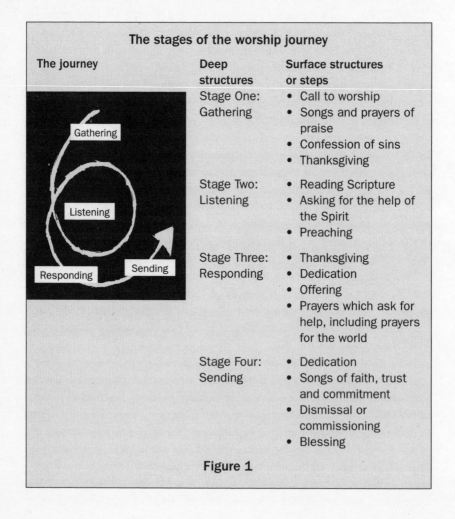

| The stages of the worship journey | | |
|---|---|---|
| **The journey** | **Deep structures** | **Surface structures or steps** |
| | Stage One: Gathering | • Call to worship<br>• Songs and prayers of praise<br>• Confession of sins<br>• Thanksgiving |
| | Stage Two: Listening | • Reading Scripture<br>• Asking for the help of the Spirit<br>• Preaching |
| | Stage Three: Responding | • Thanksgiving<br>• Dedication<br>• Offering<br>• Prayers which ask for help, including prayers for the world |
| | Stage Four: Sending | • Dedication<br>• Songs of faith, trust and commitment<br>• Dismissal or commissioning<br>• Blessing |

**Figure 1**

Such a view of worship may seem, at first glance, very complicated – but it really isn't. It gives you a tool which will help you plan creatively. If you only concentrate on the surface structures, the individual items, you may be lost in a mass of detail and find it difficult to plan the sequence of these (many) events. If you think instead of the stages of a journey and the places which need to be visited at each stage (gathering, listening, responding and sending), you have a framework in which to fit the various items in the service. If you decide to vary the order of the stages (the deep structures) then, provided there is a logic and good reason for the change, you can do so. The individual items will, of course, move with the stage to which it belongs, but you may need to think carefully how you move from one stage to the next. This pattern will work for most things you want to do with or within a service and it should help you plan and lead effective worship.

Now, before we look at the possibilities for each act within the worship event, let's pause for a culture warning!

## A matter of taste

Sometimes Christians disagree over worship. In the USA they even talk about 'worship wars'! There are two things I want to suggest about this depressing situation. First, the cause of such disagreements needs to be clearly seen as resulting from those who are disagreeing rather than from the worship which they themselves see as the cause. Let me explain. I am often asked about these conflicts over worship as though, as a supposed worship 'expert', I can give an expert answer. My only reply is as a pastor – the conflict comes from people asserting what they want over against what other people want. The problem is largely a pastoral and an ethical one, and people would do well to read some of the apostle Paul's letters, where he appeals to his readers to be forbearing towards one another and put other people's needs before their own! For example, immediately before he quotes the song of the servant king, Paul writes,

> Do nothing from selfish ambition or conceit, but in humility regard others as better than yourselves. Let each of you look not to your own interests, but to the interests of others. Let the same mind be in you that was in Christ Jesus . . .
>
> (Philippians 2.3–5)

My other observation about such disagreements is that people often confuse spiritual sincerity with matters of musical taste. Traditional hymns and contemporary music songs each have a contribution to make in worship. It's not a matter of either/or but of both/and. Yet often champions of one or the other will argue that their favoured musical genre is somehow more spiritual than the other. 'Hymns are too dry' or 'Songs are too superficial'. Such views seem to miss the point. That point is an important one for the leader of worship as we ask how each resource can contribute to meaningful worship. Let's not confuse syncopated rhythms with heartfelt devotion, or traditional tunes with lack of sincerity.

Hymns and songs have much to offer and we shall explore their respective potential when we come to Chapters 10 and 11. For now, I want to underline the value of each when it is well used and to suggest that the patterns and shapes of worship offer a framework within which we can make appropriate choices about what and when to sing. The examples which follow in this chapter will use a breadth of material. Leaders sometimes need to encourage congregations to move beyond their comfort zone and to explore cultural resources for worship which are less familiar. This may include introducing hymns where songs are usually sung, or songs where only hymns are common – or drawing on worship material from other parts of the world or from other Christian traditions.

If we return to the dynamic picture of worship as a journey, then we can see the individual units such as a song or a prayer as relating to one another in a particular way. We will not primarily see them as building blocks where one rests on top of another (that's too static) but as stepping stones which help us to move through the service. One leads to another, and that is how we move through the items within a main section, as well as helping us to move from one section to the next. But stepping stones must be carefully positioned. If they are spaced too far apart, those on the journey will not be able to make the leap from one to another. If they are too close together, the steps are easy, but the journey does not make great progress. So, as we look at the different stages of the journey, we will use this image of stepping stones to see whether we have the right things in place.

## Stage One: Gathering

Let's think for a moment about what needs to happen in this opening part of worship.

We need to encourage the members of the congregation to focus on God and to respond to what they know of God's goodness and 'Godness'. The congregation has gathered at God's invitation and in response to what God has done. In the previous chapter we thought about worship as dialogue, and so whatever we say to God, there is always the sense that it is in response to God. How can we best convey this: that all are welcome and that they are welcomed and called by God?

Praise and thanksgiving will be important – praising God for who he is, and thanking God for what he has done. This can be expressed in different ways, but the focus at this point in the service (in hymns, prayers and songs) is on God, and all God has done. Often, the confessing of our sins will be an important part of our opening worship because the more we focus on God and God's love, the more aware we become of our own sinfulness and lack of love. The assurance of our forgiveness is an important step towards being ready to listen to God's word and so is a stepping stone between focusing on ourselves and being ready and able to be open to God's word and God's Spirit. There may, however, be some services where a prayer of confession comes later in the service, perhaps as a response to the readings and the sermon.

---

### Exercise

Look at these different ways a service might begin. What might the advantages and disadvantages of each be?

| Call to worship | Welcome | Notices |
|---|---|---|
| Hymn of praise | Song of celebration | Song of praise |
| Prayer of thanksgiving | Prayer of praise | Brief prayer about God's grace |
| Hymn of thanksgiving | Song of praise | Songs of thanksgiving |
| All-age talk | Silence | |
| Song | Prayer of confession | Brief prayer |
| | Assurance of pardon | Song of devotion |
| | | Open prayer |

Write out a 'typical' beginning of a service from your church. How does it compare with these three examples?

---

Silence and open prayer are different ways to allow the congregation space to offer their own prayers and praise to God. An all-age talk introduces another route through worship. It acknowledges the diversity of the gathered congregation and introduces the theme of the service in a way which celebrates the presence of children and young people. A song might well offer a 'mini response' to this talk and lead to the point where, in many churches, the children leave for their own groups while the rest of the congregation continues its worship journey in the sanctuary.

This gathering for worship will be expressed in different ways in different worship styles, but the movement should be the same. So, in Figure 2 you can see how a fairly traditional service will enable the movement in this stage of the journey to take place. The welcome will make people feel relaxed and – yes – welcome – so that they can focus on worship. The call to worship, usually a passage of Scripture, reminds people that they gather at God's invitation and because of God's goodness and love.

> ### Act One: Gathering
>
> ### Style 1
>
> *Congregation stand for the call to worship, hymn and song.*
>
> - Welcome
> - Call to worship
> - Hymn of praise
> - Prayer of confession
> - Assurance of forgiveness
> - All-age talk
> - Song
>
> ### Figure 2

The hymn of praise is an appropriate response to having been reminded about who God is. Confession is a natural thing to want to do after facing up to God and ourselves. The assurance of forgiveness leads us on into a worship service where we are able to meet with God because we have been forgiven. This progression moves from God, to the worshippers, to a resolution of the tension created by thinking of God and ourselves in the same breath. Thus confession and forgiveness bring us to a place where our worship can continue. This way of plotting worship places a premium on our awareness of the greatness of God and our need of God's grace.

In Figure 3, we see how this gathering journey might be undertaken in a congregation where the culture of worship songs is the main expression of worship. The whole section is seen, planned and experienced as a continuum and the congregation stands throughout. In this style the congregation has more to 'say' as there is more singing, while the leader's prayers are links between the songs which focus and guide the worship through a progression of thoughts and actions – praise – celebration of salvation – thanksgiving – devotional response. Here momentum is important because the style encourages emotional engagement and the movement of worship seeks to lead the congregation into a greater degree of intensification through its ongoing, active participation. This engagement is partly expressed and supported through the continued standing of the congregation, as well as through the skilful nudging forward of the worship made possible by the brief but focused prayers of the leader. The songs themselves in this style of service can be important stepping stones, and so should be chosen carefully.

The culture of each of these styles provides a distinct way of plotting a journey through various worship actions. The illustrations demonstrate how forward planning on the part of the leader is very important, whichever style is utilized. The leader needs to plan this movement so that the congregation can be led along the journey which begins with its gathering and pays attention to the greatness and goodness of God. The journey continues and so we now shift our attention to the second stage of the service.

> **Act One: Gathering**
>
> **Style 2**
>
> *Congregation stands throughout this section.*
>
> - Welcome
> - Song of praise
> - Brief prayer acknowledging God's grace
> - Song celebrating salvation through Jesus Christ
> - Brief prayer of thanksgiving
> - Devotional song of adoration
> - Silence
> - Open prayer or prayer asking for God's help as we continue to worship
>
> **Figure 3**

## Stage Two: Listening

We have seen that the worship event is a meeting between God and the congregation. At the heart of this meeting is the time when the worshippers pay particular attention to Scripture. The individual worshippers will probably hope to learn something from this activity, but the main point of reading Scripture in worship is not an educational one. We don't read Scripture primarily as the record of God speaking in the past, but as a means through which God can speak afresh to this congregation on this day. Yes, the Holy Spirit has inspired the apostle Paul, the gospel writers, the prophets and other biblical writers. But here – in worship on this day – our prayer is that the Holy Spirit will inspire us. Through our reading, and through the exploration and application of the preacher, our hope, indeed, our expectation, is that God will address us.

This is why the diagram of the worship journey is in the shape of a spiral. The congregation gathers, not only in the sense of assembling together in one place, but gathers around the word of God. While it is true that God sometimes meets us in other parts of worship – in praise, or acts of forgiveness or dedication – God steadfastly meets us as we prayerfully and with anticipation open his word. Readers, worship leaders and preachers must do all they can to help this process but, in the end, it is the sovereign work of God's Spirit that enables this to happen. What we should do is try to do our best! We open ourselves to God, with a readiness to listen, understand and be obedient and as we listen again to voices from the past God speaks to us today.

Of course, all this is centred on Jesus Christ. The New Testament passes on to us the story of his coming among us and of God's forming of a community of his followers, the church. The Old Testament presents us with God's creative and redeeming work in the story of Israel, but it is Christian Scripture because it also prepares us, as the world has been prepared, for the coming of Christ. As Christians, we gather and pray 'in the name of Jesus', but the central stage of the worship journey is our re-engaging with all that God has done and shown in Jesus Christ. We gather around the word so that God might meet us through the one who shared our humanity in life and death, that we might know and possess the hope of glory.

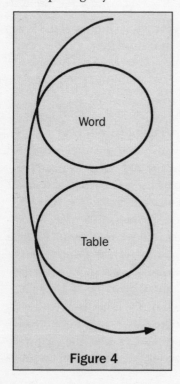

**Figure 4**

I need to qualify this, or at least expand what I have just said. This book is mainly dealing with the kind of Sunday worship which is experienced week by week by most free church and evangelical congregations: that is, worship which does not usually include the Lord's Supper, or Holy Communion. For large parts of the world Church, especially Roman Catholic, Orthodox, Anglican and Lutheran churches, Sunday worship reaches its climax in the Eucharist, and many would want to see the sharing of bread and wine as the central moment when God encounters the congregation. When free churches celebrate the Lord's Supper as part of Sunday worship, I would want to re-draw the diagram so that the spiral has two loops – we gather around the word of God and we gather around the Lord's Table (Figure 4). Both these events have been given to us as 'means of grace', where God promises to come close to us. He speaks to us his words of grace through Scripture and he meets us in grace at the table.

We shall explore the Lord's Supper in a later chapter, but, for now, we are focusing on that non-eucharistic worship which is the regular worship of most free church and evangelical congregations – most Sundays; that is, worship which centres around the reading, preaching of, and responding to, God's word in Scripture.

So in this stage of worship, how might we proceed? What are to be the likely stepping stones? In most churches this stage will mainly mean the Bible reading and the sermon, though the different local ways of doing things will vary. Figure 5 offers two parallel examples. The first represents a more traditional or liturgical approach, while the second is what you might find in more charismatic congregations. Each has its own integrity and both demonstrate that there is a shared hope that the reading and the sermon will offer opportunities to hear God's word addressed to that particular congregation. Both indicate the need for God's help on the part of the preacher – and both could indicate the desire for God's help for everyone as they listen for God's word.

---

### Stage Two – Listening

| Example One | Example Two |
|---|---|
| • Bible reading(s) by someone other than the preacher | |
| • Hymn asking for the help of the Holy Spirit | • Prayer for the preacher led by another |
| • Brief prayer by the preacher | • Bible read by preacher |
| • Sermon | • Sermon |

### Figure 5

---

All that has been said about this stage has indicated a high expectation that God will address the congregation. Such an important happening must elicit a response of some kind and so we move on to the next stage of the worship journey, But, because the response stage and the sending stage are often linked or run into one another, we shall be dealing with these two stages together.

## Stages Three and Four: Responding and sending

If we meet with God and are open to his word addressing us, then there must be some kind of response. That response will be different for different people and for different occasions, but response there needs to be. We may be called to trust God more, dedicate our lives afresh, offer for Christian service, be more honest in our praying, more loving in our relating, or more ambitious in our believing. We may be called to repent of a wrong attitude or past action, we may be invited to accept God's forgiveness and transforming power in our lives, or we may be called to trust God's grace and follow Jesus Christ for the first time. The list is almost endless, but what isn't an option is no response at all.

Perhaps the worst words a preacher can hear are, 'So what?' As we shall see, the preacher should preach for a response, and the worship leader should plan appropriate items of worship to follow the sermon so that the congregation can be helped in its response. Of course, we cannot assume that God asks the same response of everyone. There will need to be an openness in the worship planning so that a variety of responses from different members of the congregation will be possible within the same communal activity such as a prayer. However, there will usually be a core theme to the sermon which may well be the primary cue for a response on the part of the congregation, though we still need to leave opportunity for a range of personal responses.

For example, the sermon might lead to an evangelistic invitation for people to become Christians for the first time. What about all the people in the congregation who are already Christians? Well, the prayer needs to include a prompt for them to renew their faith and rededicate themselves to following Jesus Christ more closely and loving God more wholeheartedly. Or let's suppose that the theme of the sermon has been God's healing, and individuals have been invited to offer themselves for prayer for healing. There will be many people present who feel no need for healing, so they need to be encouraged to pray for others they know who need healing – or they may be invited to examine themselves to see if there are hurts from the past, or wrong attitudes which need God's healing touch.

There needs to be both focus and fudge! On the one hand there should be clear direction and opportunity for response to what is believed to be the main thrust of the sermon. On the other hand, the worship leader needs to be sensitive to the fact that the congregation is diverse and has diverse needs. Often this will be a matter of nuance, where an extra phrase is added to a prayer, or a time of silence is given for people to respond from their own situation.

One way of achieving this 'diversity with focus' is to clarify what the theme might in fact be. A sermon which results in an evangelistic challenge could be seen as being about people becoming Christians – then an invitation offered to existing Christians is seen as a kind of spin-off. It would be better, though, to see the core theme as in fact the proclamation of God's grace and the salvation which is offered in Christ. Then those who are not yet Christians can be invited to respond appropriately by putting their trust in Christ, and those who are existing Christians can respond by giving thanks for God's grace and rededicate themselves to his service, or ask for the renewing of their faith through the work of the Holy Spirit.

So what shape might these two last sections take? Again, it will vary according to the worship culture and the circumstances. Figure 6 offers two examples. There are, of course, many ways in which the response might be expressed, and we shall look at some of those in Chapter 16. What is important is that the worship leader sees his or her role to be that of providing opportunity for the members of the congregation to make their personal responses to God. Sensitivity is needed to ensure that people are not manipulated, and do not feel as though they are being manipulated. There is a fine line between speaking on behalf of a congregation and putting words into their mouths inappropriately. We must not exert pressure or make people do what we want them to do so that we can feel that the worship has been successful – whatever that means! The worship leader is called to serve, and that spirit of service must be particularly evident in this late and sensitive stage of the service.

---

### Stages Three and Four – Responding and Sending

| Example One | Example Two |
|---|---|
| • Hymn offering a response to the sermon | • Prayer from preacher following sermon |
| • Prayers which take further the congregation's varied responses | • Song |
| • Offertory and prayer | • Closing prayer and benediction |
| • Closing hymn | • Opportunity for individuals to come forward for prayer |
| • Dismissal and blessing | |

**Figure 6**

---

Of course, a most important part of our response to God is returning to our daily lives inspired and committed to serve God in the world. In Chapter 5, we noticed the importance of the joins between worship and the rest of life. This is usually expressed in the form of a dismissal or commissioning and is accompanied by a blessing or an assurance of the continuing presence of God. It is the 'sending' stage of the service, and has a particular importance in negotiating the return to daily living. People don't only cross the threshold of the church building when the worship event ends, they cross the threshold between focused prayer and practical action, between the explicit presence of God in worship and the world in which God's presence is not obvious in the same way.

Speaking personally, I believe that this closing phase of the service is vitally important and should have a sense of drama. My reservation about the second example in Figure 6 is that there may well be no negotiated transition for the congregation. It is not enough to sing a song, say the grace and offer prayer for individuals! We should send them out with words of commission and blessing in their ears and a renewed trust in God in their hearts! Here is one example of how this might be expressed:

*At the close of the final hymn, and with the congregation still standing, the minister says:*

Go into God's world as witnesses to the love of Christ;
and the blessing of God, Father, Son and Holy Spirit
be with you all. AMEN

### Exercise

Write three different sets of words for the end of a service (you could use a book of prayers for inspiration).

Would these endings be more appropriate in services with different themes?

This is not simply the end of the worship event, it is the beginning of a new week when these Christians will be hard pressed to be loyal to Jesus and need to be open to seeing God's love at work in places that don't acknowledge God, let alone God's love. They need all the help they can get, and the response and sending sections of the service help them not only to make connections between prayer and action, but to see God as the Lord of all. Notice also that the blessing above speaks of the fullness of God as Father, Son and Spirit, something it is important to hold on to.

In this chapter we have looked at the different stages of the service and tried to see how the congregation can be helped to engage with this wonderful journey. There are so many ways of covering the ground, and we have looked at only a few. Be adventurous and try different patterns. What is important is that the plans you make have an integrity, an inner logic and a natural way of tackling the theme of a particular service. Good travelling!

---

### Exercise

At the end of Chapter 6, I suggested you use the pieces of paper you had been working with to make a service on a theme of *hope, God's mercy, forgiveness, creation, or peace.*

Choose another theme and repeat the exercise, this time ensuring that the four stages we have talked about in this chapter are clearly marked. How does this change the shape of your service?

# 8

# Praying together: what and when?

Aim: To understand something of the nature and place of prayer in worship.

Prayer is an activity in which we communicate with God and God communicates with us. In worship, we pray together and it is the job of the leader to enable this to happen. Leading public prayer is different from praying in private as, when we are entrusted with leading others in worship, our main responsibility is to enable the members of the congregation to pray in ways which are helpful and appropriate for them. The proper place for our own prayers is in our times of personal devotion, not when we are standing in front of other people with the intention of leading them. This is one reason why leading worship is a ministry, a service to God and to others. We sacrifice our own needs and desires in order to serve others in helping them to pray. While we must lead with integrity and be honest as people who lead others in prayer, our own personal concerns are less important here than the needs of the congregation.

Here are two aims for the worship leader:

1   To lead prayers which in their content express Christian faith, are appropriate to the congregation and are related to the concerns of the particular worship service.
2   To lead in such a way as to enable the individual members of the congregation to pray together and for each of them to make the prayers their own.

## In the name of Jesus

Both of these aims are vital. To start with, it is very important that the prayers we offer are Christian prayers. What I mean by this is that they are based on Christian truths and that they express Christian sentiments. When we end a prayer with words such as 'through Jesus Christ our Lord', we are not just signing off with a traditional formula, we are doing something very important.

First, we are expressing our belief that our prayers are offered to God because of the relationship with God which is made possible through the atoning work of Jesus Christ on the cross. He is our high priest, and it is through him that our prayers come to the Father. Second, and more relevant here, our prayers are offered in the name of Jesus, that is, in the Spirit of Jesus. Our prayers are Christian not only because they are uttered by us, who are Christians, but because they have the character of Jesus. In other words, our prayers need to be Christ-like in the things we say and the way that we say them. Sometimes, when people are agonizing about what they should do in a particular situation, they ask, 'What would Jesus do?' When we are preparing to lead worship, we should ask, 'What would Jesus pray?' Of course, many of our prayers are actually about Jesus, so this observation is only a general guide – but it is particularly helpful when we come to pray for the world. We need to look at the world 'through the eyes of Christ' as we decide what we are going to pray about and what we are going to ask for.

When we are leading others in prayer we are, in effect, putting words in their mouths – and desires in their hearts. It is not only, or even mainly, through sermons or education programmes that people learn their faith. Prayers in worship play a large part in shaping their spirituality, as do songs and hymns. These prayers inform what they know about God, and influence what they believe. Because of this, it is important that the prayers we utter on their behalf represent orthodox Christian views about

God. From time to time we need to undertake a spiritual health check on our prayers – do they reflect God's love shown to us in Jesus and do they encourage hope in God and confidence in his gospel promises?

From a practical point of view, it may be helpful when we start to lead others in prayer to rely on some written prayers from a reliable source, or to write out our own prayers so that we might look at their content and 'feel'. There are some resource books listed at the end of this book which you may find helpful. As we shall see, we don't have to choose between written prayers or our own spontaneous prayers. Both can have a proper place in worship. However, using the prayers of others can help us to find 'a Christian voice' for our own prayers. Even after forty years of leading others in worship, I still use written prayers as well as composing prayers in my own words – both in writing before worship begins and 'on the spot', in worship itself. It's not either/or but both/and.

## Praying together

When we are leading other people in prayer, we are trying to relate to them in two distinct but related ways. On the one hand, we are trying to lead each worshipper in prayer as each person needs to come before God with sincerity of purpose and openness of heart, relying upon God's mercy and seeking God's help. The way we lead needs to take account of the people who have gathered for worship. For example, in an all-age service we are likely to use simple words and concepts which include the younger worshippers and help them to pray. We will look at a congregation and try and judge what individual needs and concerns are expressed in it so that we can help in the way we lead prayer.

But we also need to remember that a congregation is just that – a congregation. It is not only a collection of individuals but a community of people who have gathered to worship God together. So we need to focus on communal concerns as well as individual needs. Sometimes I am invited to lead worship in a church other than the one I serve as pastor. It is important that I try and understand the general situation of that congregation, as well as being aware of any particular circumstances which may need to be addressed in prayer at that time.

We are called to lead this congregation in this place on this day. Wherever possible, our prayers need to reflect the specifics of the community we are entrusted with leading in prayer. What are the challenges facing this community? What are the mission needs of the neighbourhood or the issues which weigh heavily on their hearts? What does the

Scripture reading or the sermon say to this community and how can we help it to respond appropriately to God's word?

When we list the different types of prayer that are possible in a service, there are two different ways in which we can sort them. On the one hand, we can talk about different types of prayer with regard to their **content**, what the prayers say or do (praise, thanksgiving etc). On the other hand, we can sort prayers into types of prayer **style** (prayer book, spontaneous prayer, responsive prayer, etc.). In other words – what we say and how we say it. Before going on, in the following chapter, to look at the different ways in which we can express these prayers, we shall first look at the different types of prayer according to their content and what we believe we are doing when we offer them.

## What we say

There are, of course, many things we could say in prayer. Sometimes people will pray long prayers in which they say many different kinds of things. In previous centuries, free church worship used to contain what was called 'the long prayer' and sometimes it was very long indeed. There are even records of it going on for the best part of an hour, while 20–30 minutes was quite common! The long prayer was a rambling address to God which included everything from praise and thanksgiving to requests for help in difficult circumstances. It was a monologue on behalf of the congregation, a kind of 'stream of consciousness' way of praying which reflected a time when people were used to listening to long prayers – and even longer sermons!

However, shorter prayers are to be commended for use today: short prayers with a clear focus which will help the congregation in two main ways:

1  A short prayer with a single theme will aid concentration on the part of those listening and thus help them to make the prayer their own.
2  A short prayer with a single theme will help the service develop in such a way as to enable the congregation to journey through different moods and actions. In this way, the prayers, as well as being significant in themselves, also become stepping stones within the service.

Of course, you can link several short prayers together if you want to lead the congregation through several actions in a short space of time. For example, you might offer a single prayer which includes praise, confession of our sins and thanksgiving for God's promise of forgiveness.

Alternatively, you might want to offer prayers of intercession for different situations and then offer a prayer of trust in God or an expression of thanksgiving for past blessings.

Some different types of prayer are listed in Figure 1 according to their content and the action they are expressing.

| What we pray | |
| --- | --- |
| • invocation | in which we ask (invoke) God to help us in our worship and praying. This will often come at the beginning of a service or before a sermon or a time of silent prayer. |
| • praise | in which we acknowledge who God is and offer our adoration. Again, this will often come early in a service when we focus on God as the only reality worthy of our worship, but prayers of adoration can be appropriate at almost any point in the service. |
| • confession | in which we acknowledge and confess our sinfulness and ask for God's forgiveness. This is an important feature and is too often omitted from evangelical worship. Confession is a sign of spiritual realism when we acknowledge what we are really like and ask for God's help. It is also an important expression of the gospel of forgiveness and the grace of God. This can come early in the service or, for example, in response to the sermon or, sometimes, at the beginning of the Lord's Supper. |
| • lament | in which we complain to God that things are not as they should be, yet continue to express our trust in God. Here we struggle to trust while expressing what we feel about injustice and the wrongs of the world – just like some of the psalms. |
| • thanksgiving | in which we thank God for what God has done and what God has given us. This prayer also helps us to view the world gratefully, recognizing that everything comes from God. Again, this can come at almost any point in a service, though it will be thematically linked to the things which have just preceded it. So, for example, it could follow a sermon which has celebrated the faithfulness of God, or the testimony of a person who has spoken of God working in their lives – as well as offering general thanks for God's goodness towards us. |
| **Figure 1** | |

| | |
|---|---|
| • intercession | in which we pray for the world and for other people. This is an act of love and an expression of trust in God. Often it will come after the sermon, as we respond to what God's word has said to us, or it may come earlier in the service as we pray for concerns regarding the state of the world. |
| • petition | in which we pray for ourselves and ask for God's help. This kind of prayer would normally come later in a service, though we could perhaps occasionally plan a service where such prayers were offered near the beginning if we wanted to start with our concerns so we could 'deal' with them and then move on to listen to God. |
| • dedication and commitment | in which we give ourselves to God in recommitment and in which we dedicate ourselves for God's service. This prayer of consecration is very important because it expresses our worship of God in a way which embraces the whole of who we are – it also makes the link between worship and the rest of our lives. |
| • offering | in which we dedicate things (e.g. money) to God. If the collection of money is offered in a prayer it is good to include the dedication of ourselves and the life and witness of the congregation to God as well. |
| • blessing | in which we seek God's blessing on our lives and the lives of the congregation. This will normally come at the close of the service as the congregation is commissioned to live in the world as servants of Christ. But prayers of blessing can come at various points in the service, such as the commissioning of someone for a ministry or task in the church. |

**Figure 1 (cont.)**

This list simply itemizes the different concerns we pray about and the various things that we 'do' in prayer. It doesn't lay down rigid rules about the order or sequence in which these prayers should be arranged. Although we might think, for example, that worship should begin with praise, there is a lot of flexibility as to the order in which we pray. Chapters 6 and 7 have explored how the worship service might be designed, but for now, let's look at some of the possible ways in which these prayers might relate to one another.

### Exercise

You are leading worship on Sunday. The two readings which have been chosen are Ezekiel 37.1–14 and John 11.17–44. Write or sketch out some prayers of the different types listed in Figure 1, which are inspired by the readings and pick up some of their themes.

Which were the easiest and hardest to write? Why do you think that was? Were these the types of prayer that were most and least familiar?

Which of these prayers would you find it easiest to use in your own church?

## How and when we say it

Different kinds of services will tend to need different kinds of prayers. A service which comprises mainly the singing of worship songs (and in which the congregation's praying is mainly expressed through those songs) will require a different style of prayer from a service in which the congregation will expect to pray through saying some of the words of the prayers together. Here are three different ways in which prayers can relate to the rest of the service.

### 1 Dynamic flow

This is when there is a logical sequence to the various prayers, which in turn structures the worship service or the prayer time.

The most common example of this is the acrostic ACTS, where one type of prayer leads to the next.

- **Adoration** – when we focus on how wonderful God is and offer praise and express delight at being in the presence of this loving and gracious God.
- **Confession** – when we recognize our own sinfulness, and the sin of the world to which we each contribute, and ask for God's forgiveness. It is sometimes followed by an 'assurance of forgiveness', pronounced by the worship leader (often expressed in words of Scripture, such as 1 John 1.9), which reminds the congregation of the gospel truth that God forgives those who truly repent and seek his forgiveness.
- **Thanksgiving** – when we acknowledge how everything comes from God and that God's generosity is the foundation of our lives. We

especially give thanks for the gift of Jesus Christ and our redemption through his cross and resurrection.
- **Supplication** – when we ask God for things. These requests can take two forms:
  - **intercession** – when we pray for others,
  - **petition** – when we pray for ourselves.

Can you see a flow through these prayers? We begin with focusing on God. To **adore** is to see God as the centre of our whole existence, to offer praise, love and devotion. But our awareness of God's goodness and holiness prompts us to recognize how sinful we are and how much we need God's forgiveness and help. So we **confess** our sins, and because the gospel proclaims how that forgiveness is possible through the cross and resurrection of Jesus Christ, we give **thanks** for our salvation as well as for the gift of life itself and all God's blessings. Reminded of God's loving generosity, we are encouraged to bring our requests for others and ourselves.

This could happen in one large block of prayer, though I wouldn't recommend such an indigestible way of doing things. It could happen in two prayer blocks, such as praise, confession and thanksgiving, followed later by intercession and petition. Alternatively, these aspects of prayer may be expressed in different ways during the course of a service – for example, the thanksgiving may be expressed through the congregation singing a hymn rather than through a conventional prayer led by a worship leader. In a congregation which is used to a 'contemporary praise and worship' style, the praise, confession and thanksgiving prayers may well be expressed through a sequence of songs and link prayers or Scripture sentences at the beginning of the service.

The ACTS pattern doesn't only offer a helpful flow of ideas which can shape a worship event, it also offers a health check by listing the types of prayer which a service should include if the community is to enjoy a balanced diet of worship. There may well be other kinds of prayer which ought to be included. Most services should give opportunity for a prayer of dedication or consecration as we offer ourselves to God in worship and discipleship.

> ### Exercise
>
> Write a series of short prayers that fit the ACTS pattern. Do this in a general way which might be used in any service. Then repeat the exercise in a way that would be suitable either for a Christmas or an Easter service.

ACTS isn't by any means the only pattern of praying, though many Christians would see it as the default position. Can you imagine a different dynamic flow through the prayers and events of a worship service? For example you might on occasion begin with proclamation of all that God has done and move to thanksgiving and eventually move from focusing on what God has done to who God is – adoration.

## 2  Signpost prayers

It is helpful to think of the entire service as an integrated whole, rather than simply a collection of small units such as hymns, prayers and readings. In some parts of the service, the congregation is being addressed by God or the worship leaders and at other times the congregation is addressing God, often through the worship leader acting as a representative of the congregation. These prayers are very important in focusing what is being thought about in that part of the service.

So a prayer after the sermon may not only offer a means of helping the congregation respond to the challenge of the sermon but also provide a stepping stone to what follows. Similarly, prayers at different points in the service can act as a means of highlighting what is being done and said by offering these things to God. This kind of prayer can also act as a link between various parts of the service. So if the reading follows the offering, then the prayer dedicating the offering might not only give thanks for God's generosity and dedicate the money and the lives of the congregation for God's service. It might also anticipate the reading by thanking God for the gift of Scripture, and asking for the help of the Holy Spirit to open hearts and minds to receive God's word. Similarly, in a 'worship sequence' of songs, some Bible verses and short prayers can help the worshippers through a journey of worship moments where the themes of the songs are underlined and advanced, albeit briefly.

## 3  Prayers of response

The congregation will often need opportunities to respond to what is said or done in the service. For example, the prayer at the end of the sermon may be very important, as it provides an opportunity for the congregation to respond to what has been said. There may have been words of promise or encouragement which need appropriating, or words of invitation or challenge which should not be left hanging in mid air. There may be news of a troubled world which requires us to offer up prayers, or news of the church family which prompts us to give thanks.

Now there is a sense in which all prayer is prayer of 'response'. Even an opening prayer of adoration or praise is responding to what we already know of the love and grace of God. The initiative is always God's. Verse 4.19 in 1 John announces, 'We love because he first loved us.' And we pray because first God has come to us in saving grace and sought us – Jesus' parable of the lost sheep is a powerful picture of our experience of God who comes in search of us because of love. As the title of this book suggests, we approach God in worship because God is, first, the approaching God who takes the initiative in the relationship between us. All our prayer is in response to this initiative-taking, coming-close-to-us, God.

Yet, within worship, there is an important place for seeing certain prayers as an opportunity to express our response to God – in repentance, in trust, in consecration of our lives. Our prayer, in preparing ourselves and others for worship, is that God's Spirit will change our hearts of stone into hearts of flesh (Ezekiel 36.26) so that we might respond to God's life-changing word.

Prayer is the natural way of relating to God in worship, and worship leaders should continually be asking themselves how they can articulate for the congregation an appropriate response to what is happening in the service. When do we pray? As often as possible! Many services have very little prayer and this is an issue for each worship leader to ponder.

---

### Exercise

Prayers act as stepping stones which help the congregation to journey together with God. Write down the ten different types of prayer from Figure 1 on different pieces of paper. Arrange them in different orders as if this was the flow of prayers through different services. What do you notice about the different orders? In what ways might they give a service a different feel?

Write out the ten different types again on different pieces of paper. Which of these second pieces do you think would be appropriate to add in to the flow of the first pieces, so you have two occasions of one type of prayer in one service? Which types of prayer do you think would be less appropriate to repeat during one service?

# 9

# The prayer spectrum: style and expression

Aim: To explore the different ways in which prayers may be expressed in worship.

'Variety is the spice of life', or so the saying goes. When it comes to prayer, we have seen how different prayers may be helpful at different points in a service. Once we also recognize that different congregations will have different shapes of worship then the possibilities for varied prayers become even greater.

To this range of possibilities we can then add the varieties of 'style' to be found in different congregations. There is the variety of language, with some congregations still using the Authorized (or King James) Version of the Bible, and consequently using such AV language in their prayers. Others will use contemporary language, but vary in whether they highly prize a spontaneous and 'passionate' prayer style, or whether they appreciate carefully crafted and creatively expressed written prayers. Some will want open prayer opportunities for the congregation and others will want scripted responses to give the congregation a collective voice in prayer.

It is good to remind ourselves that there are various ways in which prayer can be expressed and that such variety will be enriching for many congregations – not least, because different personalities in each congregation will find different ways of praying helpful. Let's now look at some of these options in a bit more detail.

# The prayer spectrum

Most forms of prayer in free church worship are examples of representative prayer, in which one person prays out loud on behalf of the whole congregation. We will look briefly at other forms of prayer, but it is with this sense of the worship leader being a spokesperson that we shall begin.

As we have seen, there is a big difference between praying in your own personal devotions and praying in public. It's not just that there is another audience in addition to God! When we are leading a service, we are not praying on our own behalf, but are being entrusted with leading a whole congregation in prayer. This requires empathy and imagination, as we try to put into words what we think the members of the congregation would want, or ought, to pray. So the phrases we use and the things we pray about need to be selected in order to help the congregation pray, rather than express what we personally are feeling. Of course, if we have an on-going relationship with the congregation, or if we can use our imagination and put ourselves in their shoes, then what we think would be helpful or appropriate for public prayer could well be close to what we would want to pray ourselves. But we should put the congregation first, both in the content and the style of prayer. 'What will help these particular people to pray today?' is the sort of question we should be asking.

So let's look at the various ways in which prayer can happen in worship:

## 1 Extempore prayer

A dictionary definition of 'extempore' claims that it means 'on the spur of the moment; without premeditation or preparation; without notes'. This last phrase is probably the most helpful when we are thinking of extempore prayer. The word comes originally from the Latin for 'of the time' and refers to that which is composed and delivered in a specific moment. It is not written down and is usually spontaneous in its phrasing, though not necessarily its ideas. It is 'off the cuff', and some Christians will regard this as a virtue, while others will regard it with some suspicion or nervousness. There are two main types of extempore prayer:

- **wholly spontaneous prayer** for which there has been no prior thought or planning, and
- **conceived prayer** where the framework of the prayer, or its main themes, has been planned in advance, often through personal prayer, while the final phrasing is spontaneous.

Theologically, some will see extempore prayer as an example of the person praying while relying on the leading of the Holy Spirit. Closely linked to this view may be the attitude that an informal style of speaking, coupled to spontaneity, are suggestive of sincerity and spiritual authenticity.

Sometimes people seem to think that the more rough and ready the phrasing, the more 'real' the prayer is likely to be. As a result, there can be a kind of indulging in sloppiness: 'Lord, we would just ask you, Lord that you just help us to worship you, Lord . . . '. I'm not knocking the sentiments – the desire for an approachable language to help the congregation to pray, and a concern to be sincere – but I am deeply suspicious that sincerity can be thought to be achieved through a linguistic naivety which will soon grate on the ears of the worshippers. This may be the language of personal devotion for some, and it may be accepted and honoured as the prayer expression of someone leading prayer in public for the first time, but as a continuing practice it doesn't edify many in the public arena of shared worship!

Meanwhile, we need to recognize that not all people are able to express themselves spontaneously in a coherent way that will be helpful for the congregation they are leading. If you are invited to pray in public you should not feel that you have to pray this way, though in time you may develop the gift. What is most important is that you give your best in helping the congregation to prayer appropriately. If that means writing the prayer out in full beforehand, or using pre-composed prayers written by other people, then so be it. Read on!

## 2 Written prayers

There is nothing wrong, and often much to be gained, from reading prayers from a pre-composed script, though you should read them in such a way that they sound sincere and sound like your own words, not the words of others that you are reading. Of course, you should never actually claim that the words are your own when they have been written by someone else. However, you don't usually need to attribute the prayers while leading the service, unless you want to make a special point of some kind. At all costs avoid a 'parsonic' tone of voice in which the pitch of your voice drops at the end of each line or sentence – and never read prayers as though you were indifferent to their content. You are leading the congregation in prayer: you are addressing God and enabling others to do so through your words, so read pre-composed prayers in such a way that you are praying and leading others in prayer.

Pre-composed prayers are likely to come from two main sources:

- Prayers that you write yourself, which can have all the advantages of extempore prayers in being focused on what you want to pray on behalf of a particular congregation in a particular place on a particular day; and
- Collections of prayers and services published in books, or on the Web, which often have the advantage of very careful and helpful phrasing. Most congregations and most worship leaders will benefit from using some published prayers on some occasions. Indeed, you may well find that using helpful words from other people will, in time, help you to find our own words in leading prayer.

Here is an example of a pre-composed prayer of thanks and adoration which uses language and images creatively, yet has a simplicity which will connect with many worshippers:

Living God,
we give you thanks and praise,
for you have made us and given us life,
you have redeemed us and set us free.

Loving God,
we give you thanks and praise,
for you have found us and made us your own,
named us and called us 'Beloved'.

Accompanying God,
we give you thanks and praise,
for you have promised to be with us always
and nothing can separate us from your love.

God, our God,
we love you and adore you.

(Ellis and Blyth, *Gathering for Worship*, p. 306)

---

### Exercise

Find some written prayers from a variety of different sources (books, internet, church service sheets). What strikes you about the language that is used?

In what ways is the language different from either the language of extempore prayer which you are used to, or written words you might read in another setting (newspaper, book, report etc.)?

---

## 3 Responsive prayers and litanies

Sometimes it is helpful for written prayers to be composed in such a way that some of the words can be said by the congregation rather than the worship leader. This has the advantage of giving the congregation a voice, though, of course, the words are pre-scripted. In denominations which use books of common prayer, most of the service will comprise scripted prayers to be said either by the worship leader or the congregation in a kind of dialogue. Sometimes this is called 'liturgical prayer', and we shall look at it some more in Chapter 16.

Even though you may not be leading worship in a 'liturgical' denomination, you may still want to use responsive prayers sometimes and you may either find them in a book of prayers or compose them yourself. Photocopying and the use of overhead projectors or data projectors make it easy to provide the congregation with the written words of such responses, although you will need to be aware of any copyright restrictions. You might like to find some ideas in books of prayers and then experiment yourself. If you compose the prayer yourself, it is worth thinking about which words the leader will say and which words the congregation will be invited to say. Of course, if you plan a simple, repeated response (such as *Lord, in your mercy:* **Hear our prayer**), it will not need to be written down.

Here is an extract from a responsive prayer: the words for the congregation to say are printed in bold.

Gracious God,
Rejoicing in your blessings,
Trusting in your loving care for all,
We bring you our prayers for the world . . .

We pray for people in need:
those for whom life is a bitter struggle;
those whose lives are clouded
by death or loss,
by pain or disability,
by discouragement or fear,
by shame or rejection.

*Silence*

In the lives of those in need
**Your kingdom come, O Lord,**
**Your will be done.**

We pray for those
in the circle of friendship and love around us:
children and parents;
sisters and brothers;
friends and neighbours;
and for those especially in our thoughts today . . .

*Silence*

In the lives of those we love
**Your kingdom come, O Lord,**
**Your will be done.**

We pray for the church
in its stand with the poor,
in its love for the outcast and the ashamed,
in its service to the sick and the neglected,
in its proclamation of the Gospel,
in this land and in this place.

*Silence*

In the life of your church
**Your kingdom come, O Lord,**
**Your will be done.**

Eternal God:
hear these our prayers,
the spoken and the silent,
through Jesus Christ our Lord,
to whom with you and the Holy Spirit,
be all praise and glory for ever.

(Ellis and Blyth, *Gathering for Worship*, pp. 328f.)

Another example of responsive prayer might be the use of a psalm as a prayer. If you have the Bible on computer, then copy and paste a suitable psalm into your word processor. Then space the psalm into paragraphs (ignoring the verse divisions) so that it makes sense when prayed aloud by two voices. Then decide which sections

### Exercise

Choose a Psalm and try and turn it into a responsive prayer like this.

Try the exercise again using a New Testament passage – you may need to turn the words around so they address God.

you want the congregation to say and print those in bold type. My suggestion is that you give the strongest affirmations to the congregation and that you, as the worship leader, say the cues – rather like a 'straight man' feeding a comedian, so that the comedian comes in with the punch lines.

## 4 Open prayer

One way of leading a congregation in prayer is to provide an opportunity for individuals to pray aloud so that they become temporary worship leaders! You might want to introduce such a session by suggesting certain themes for people's prayers and by closing the session by praying aloud yourself.

For practical reasons, open prayer works best in small congregations, as audibility becomes a problem in large congregations unless special arrangements are made by providing microphones at various parts of the building – and then there is a certain loss of spontaneity. But experimenting is good – provided you consult afterwards to see if people found it helpful, and modify your practice accordingly.

## 5 Group prayer

A variation on open prayer is to invite the congregation to break up into small groups of three to five people and for them to share concerns on a given theme before praying informally in those groups. This is more difficult when there are pews but, where there's a will there's a way. However, you need to be sensitive to the culture of a local church – some congregations will take to this like ducks to water, while others will want to curl up in a ball or run away!

## 6 Collects

These are short prayers of no more than one paragraph which are often found in prayer books. They are normally used as a way of rounding off or summing up a series of prayers or biddings – or even silent prayer on an agreed theme – but they can also be used as stand-alone short prayers.

Traditionally, collects comprise a number of features:

- an opening which greets God and states some particular aspect of God's character or something which God has done;
- a request based upon that particular aspect;
- a doxology, or petition in the name of Jesus.

Here is an example of the collect form written for a service at new year:

Lord of history,
to whom a thousand years are as a day:
renew us by your Holy Spirit,
that, while we have life and breath,
we may serve you with courage and hope;
through the grace of your Son,
our Saviour Jesus Christ.

(Ellis and Blyth, *Gathering for Worship*, p. 362)

If you look in a prayer book such as *Common Worship* you will recognize this framework and will soon be able to write your own if you wish. There are many beautiful and well-phrased collects which can enrich your worship – they even mix well as a way of ending extempore prayer.

## 7 Silent Prayer

It has been said that some people prefer the radio to television because the pictures are better. What is meant is that the medium of radio, like that of a novel, requires us to provide the images for the drama out of our own imagination, using memories and pictures from the past as well as ones imagined for the first time. In a similar kind of way, it is sometimes helpful to give a congregation the space needed for people to imagine and phrase their own prayers in silence. The pictures may be better than those of the worship leader – or at least the images and ideas intuitively experienced and offered to God in silent prayer might be more relevant, personal and powerful than anything which could be said from the front.

Some congregations will not be used to silent prayer and will, at first, need some help. Don't make the silences too long – but avoid the danger of not giving enough time for silence. If there are several periods of silence in a prayer time then thirty seconds each time might be the right amount. Give the congregation some prompts – this isn't a free-for-all time but corporate prayer undertaken in silence. Announce a theme and, if there are several moments of silence, then give a lead at the beginning of each. Don't be prescriptive and overpowering but suggest what they might pray about in the silence. At the end it is good to finish with a short prayer offered by the leader, and often a collect will work well – as it 'collects together' the various prayers of the congregation.

## 8 Guided meditation

This is a prayer which is not initially addressed to God but is a kind of thinking out loud by the leader in a reflective way which draws others into the imaginative line of thought.

Often this will work after a Scripture reading when the leader muses about its meaning, or speaks conversationally to God about the implication of the reading in our lives. There are many published examples of this kind of prayer which will work well in worship, but it is also good to have a go and write such a meditation yourself. Just make sure you don't lecture God, or inform him of the contents of the latest news bulletin! Sometimes it can be a mixture of thinking out loud, a soliloquy, interspersed with verses of Scripture and some bits addressed directly to God.

## 9 Multi-sensory prayer

Sometimes words, and even silence, cannot express what needs to be expressed. Contemporary society seems more open to ritual or symbolic actions than it has been for some time. As a result, prayers in worship could sometimes include symbolic actions – either on the part of the leader or on the part of the congregation.

A time of prayer might include the opportunity for members of the congregation to come forward and light a candle as a symbolic way of identifying with what has been prayed on their behalf, or as a way of expressing their own silent prayer contribution to the service – perhaps they might name a person or situation as they light the candle and invite others to share in prayer with them for that concern.

On another occasion you might want to use the symbols of light and darkness with the use of candles. Or you might invite the congregation to come forward, to choose a pebble and together construct a cairn, a sign of faith and trust in the Lord who calls us to journey with him.

## 10 Prayer ministry

This is not strictly a way of leading prayer within a worship service as it usually happens immediately afterwards. You may wish to offer the opportunity for individuals to come to the front of the worship area, or some other suitable place, during the singing of the closing hymn or immediately after the benediction so that a member of an appointed prayer team might pray with them. This isn't corporate worship but it is a pastoral response to things which have happened during corporate worship and may be very helpful both for the individuals concerned and for others as they see this prayer activity continuing.

## Finally . . .

To lead others in prayer is a great responsibility, but don't be overawed by it, because God calls ordinary people to do this. Try to be imaginative in the language and methods you use, but, above all, be sensitive to the needs of the people who have been entrusted to your leadership. And if in doubt – pray!

---

### Exercise

Think about your usual experiences of worship, whether you often lead worship or are usually led by others. Which of the above styles of prayer are you most familiar with? Which do you use / are used frequently in your church, which occasionally and which hardly ever? What do you think the effects or implications might be of using just some styles of prayer?

Now take the opportunity to experiment. Next time you lead worship (or offer to lead some prayers in your church) try something new, and use a style with which you are less familiar. (It is probably worth just trying one new thing at a time!) Make sure you reflect yourself on how it went and also try and ask for feedback from some of the congregation.

---

# 10

# Singing: why and when?

Aim: To explore the purpose of congregational singing and its place in worship.

'He who sings prays twice.' I first came across this quotation from St Augustine on a Christian poster some years ago – and I'm still not sure what it means! Perhaps it is that when we sing a hymn or song we pray with words as we sing aloud and we pray with the heart as we hear the words we have just sung. Perhaps it is that the words we sing are more memorable than words we speak, so we tend to sing them to ourselves afterwards and thus repeat the prayer. Perhaps it

> ### Exercise
>
> 'He who sings prays twice.'
> *St Augustine*
>
> What do *you* think Augustine meant by this?

means something else – but its haunting and elusive profundity reminds us that music, and singing in particular, has been a central feature of much Christian worship. Why is this?

## Why sing?

In his book, *The Singing Thing*, John Bell offers ten reasons why we sing. First, he says it's 'because we can'. Singing is natural, like snapping your fingers or laughing at a joke. It's true that some can't, but they usually

82

have a sense of missing out on something which seems to come naturally to most people and most cultures. Second, singing helps us to express and develop group identity, as groups have particular songs they enjoy singing or which express something they believe about their community. At the same time, the rhythms of music help us to utter words together which we might find far harder to simply say together. Third, singing helps express and, fourth, trigger our emotions just as they help us to flesh out the depth of meaning in certain words, and the association of favourite tunes with particular hymns reinforces this.

Fifth, John Bell claims that songs often evoke memories and help us to revisit the past. Then, sixth, there are many songs which simply tell a story and tell it well. Seventh, singing helps shape the future as it draws us into the hopes and dreams which the songs express. John Bell comments, 'Singing is a hearing and seeing and, above, all, doing activity. It requires us to take into ourselves and circulate through our system words and music which others have written and, for a shorter or longer period, to make these our own.'

Eighth, in some cultures, singing helps people work and in worship singing can help the congregation to share actively in the work of worshipping God. Then, ninth, singing uses our creativity. The song is just a collection of dots and words on a page until it is brought alive in performance, and each set of musicians and each gathering of people will bring their unique combination of gifts and experiences to that performance. Finally, when we sing we give something of ourselves. When we sing we make ourselves vulnerable – there is always the possibility that we will go out of tune and just utter a croak – and our singing is a gift of ourselves to others and to God.

Now this very brief summary does not do justice to John Bell's book, which I heartily recommend. It misses out the human stories and leaves out all the jokes. But as a very brief list, it does at least suggest the many different ways in which singing can be seen as a powerful influence and the effect it can have on people in many different situations and cultures. We need first to understand singing as a basic human activity which expresses and gives depth to our lives, if we are to understand its significance for worship.

## Singing in worship

While I think that John Bell's ten points all have something to contribute to our understanding, I want now to concentrate my reflections on just a few of them.

## 1 Singing helps us to say things together

This is very important both for the experience of the worshippers, as they do something communally, and for those who are leading and planning worship. Quite apart from what the hymns and songs say, or the mood they evoke or express, congregational singing enables the congregation to have a voice – and to have a shared voice. Singing helps people say something together – to praise together, to give thanks together, to celebrate or confess together. It is no wonder that congregational singing has increased as a proportional part of worship services in many churches in recent years. As cultural changes lead to less willingness to be part of a passively attentive crowd and more inclination to be involved in the gathering, singing provides a primary way in which this can be affected.

Singing provides two particular opportunities for the worship leader. First, it becomes an important way of enabling the whole congregation to participate collectively in the service. So in most 'non-liturgical' churches, hymns and songs are the main way in which the congregation is enabled to say things together. Of course, other parts of the service are also communal, but they tend to be led by one person speaking representatively on behalf of everyone present.

In singing together we are expressing something very important. Not only is this togetherness useful, in the sense that it provides a practical means of helping the members of the congregation to worship together in an 'active' way, but it is also theologically significant. The gospel of Jesus Christ is about the reconciliation of all things – fellowship with God and fellowship with one another (see Colossians 1.20 and Ephesians 2.13–22). When we sing, the togetherness of our utterance, the unity of our rhythm and the richness of our harmony are all an expression of our being a reconciled community and an anticipation of that greater oneness of which we shall be a part one day.

Second, in congregational singing, each worshipper speaks, or rather sings (!), for his or her own self. 'O LORD, open my lips, and my mouth will declare your praise' (Psalm 51.15). When we sing, it is our own mouths which declare – not a representative on our behalf. It is a participative activity and provides worship leaders with a way of planning and enabling individuals to be more actively involved in the worship service. Perhaps this is most evident when a song provides a means of people responding to the gospel and a vehicle through which they can dedicate or rededicate themselves to God. Better than silent prayer, they sing out loud and give something of themselves through the utterance of the song and their own singing of it. But this participation is also important in other aspects of worship, such as praise and thanksgiving, where the worshippers participate openly in these important actions towards God.

## 2 Singing reaches parts that words alone often can't touch

For centuries, ordinary Christians have often found themselves expressing their faith by quoting hymns. It is as though the combination of poetry and music reaches deeper into their emotional engagement with the spiritual realities which are being described or expressed than prose (ordinary sentences) can ever do. For example, take these words of Charles Wesley, from his hymn 'And can it be':

'Tis mystery all: the immortal dies!
Who can explore his strange design?

The worshippers are encouraged not only to contemplate the wonderful redemption made possible through the death of Christ, but to proclaim and reflect upon the wonder of God being on the cross. The congregation is then invited to celebrate the life-changing work of God's forgiveness in their lives:

Long my imprisoned spirit lay
Fast bound in sin and nature's night:
Thine eye diffused a quickening ray –
I woke, the dungeon flamed with light,
My chains fell off, my heart was free,
I rose, went forth, and followed thee.

Here is image after image, expressing the difference God can make in our lives. How much more powerful and involving is this than saying it in descriptive prose and, when it is sung with a strong and enjoyable tune, there can be a great sense of communal rejoicing.

Singing has this capability to touch hearts as well as minds in communal worship. When we add to this the way that hymns and songs can be so memorable, and that people will often associate particular songs with significant moments in their lives, then we have a potent mix indeed. Hymns sung at funerals, songs sung at times of personal crisis, and either sung in moments of spiritual growth and commitment, all combine to illustrate the power of singing. But this very power requires a health warning for the worship leader. First, we need to recognize this potential and use it wisely, carefully choosing hymns and songs which express and move forward the theme of the service, rather than simply picking some golden oldies or fashionable favourites in order to hide a lack of cohesion or preparation in the worship leading. Second, we need to recognize that this very power can lead to the use of music in manipulating the emotions of the congregation in a way which is unfair and downright unchristian. God's power is the power of the cross and the power of love. If God avoids coercion and manipulation, so should we. There is a fine line between using music in a way which provides support and atmosphere, and using it to play on the emotions and getting people to do things which they would not otherwise do. The ends do not justify the means, even when people seem to be coming to faith for the first time.

## 3 Singing encourages involvement and self-giving

Song writing is clearly a very creative activity, both in forming the lyrics and composing the music. But much creativity is also in evidence when songs are performed. Many congregations will have musicians who, either singly or, more commonly, as groups, contribute to the worship of the community. Singers and instrumentalists have much to offer, and this area of service provides an important means for a number of people to contribute to the leading of worship. If you are a worship leader you should encourage these gifted helpers. Your relationship with them is very important, as good communication and empathetic co-working is vital in the leading of worship, especially when that worship is flexible in style.

Again there are a couple of health warnings. People often feel strongly about music and you need to have built a relationship of trust and mutual respect with the musicians if you are sometimes to negotiate a constructive way through potential disagreements.

We also need to remember those individuals in the congregation who say they cannot sing and who appear to be tone deaf. For them, a service with a lot of music may be something of an ordeal, and the more we use music to help the congregation as a whole, the more they may feel marginalized and unsupported. This is, of course, no reason to leave out all the music or singing, but we do need to be sensitive to such pastoral needs and find a variety of ways of enabling the congregation to express the various modes of worship.

## 4 Remember – singing is only instrumental

This point has, of course, nothing to do with instrumental accompaniment whether, organ, music group or orchestra! Something which is 'instrumental' is something which we don't use for its own sake but in order to achieve something else. Music and singing exist in worship in order to help the congregation worship. This is not an exercise in community singing and it is certainly not a concert! Music is a means to an end and we must never lose sight of that end – helping people worship God. If music gets in the way – then get rid of the music! In fact, it is a good exercise sometimes to lead a service which contains no music at all. While this has the added benefit of affirming the non-singers, it also helps us to see how music can be used (because we will wish we could have used it here or there) and encourages other forms of creativity. Visuals, the creative use of storytelling or poetry or silence – all these can help us to lead worship alongside music. But if we deliberately go on a music fast then they can come into their own in a special way.

> ### Exercise
>
> Take an order of service (either one which you have used in the recent past, or a written down order of what has happened in a service at church) and re-work it so it keeps the same meaning and impact, but without using any singing at all.
>
> What does the exercise suggest both about the ways singing can be used and also other possible alternatives?

## Hymns and songs

Each of these factors will at various times influence the planning of a service, which songs to sing and when to sing them. For example, the power of a song to encourage personal involvement may well mean that a worship leader will choose such a song at a point in a worship service where they want to encourage commitment on the part of the congregation. So a song can provide the vehicle for personal dedication and consecration. Alternatively, the power of a song to reach parts of our awareness that other forms of communication cannot, may lead to the selection of a particular song to help the congregation respond to a vision of God's greatness or sacrificial love. Such a use may also be important in enabling praise, where the combination of a strong tune and lofty words can lift a congregation into an awesome sense of God's presence and majesty.

But, for the rest of this chapter I want to look at how hymns and songs can fit into the flow of a worship event – how they can not only express great thoughts and emotions, but progress the worshippers through a series of worship actions in their encounter with God on the journey of worship. In other words, I want to look at the way that hymns and songs can act as stepping stones in the service. In order to do this we need to consider both the internal shape of a hymn or a song, and the way they might be used to advance the service itself.

People can use the words 'hymn' or 'song' in quite a flexible way. However, I want to suggest a distinction between them which, while it might not be universally accepted, I think offers a helpful way of understanding their use. Sometimes people think that the distinction is to be found in the musical style of hymns and songs – that hymns tend to have a regular metre and are sung to traditional tunes while songs tend to be sung to more contemporary music. This has some truth, but there are too many exceptions to make it a helpful distinction. For example, there are many hymns which are sung to contemporary tunes.

A better way of distinguishing between hymns and songs is to do so on the basis of their form or shape. **Hymns** tend to have a number of verses and the train of thought is a linear one. This means that ideas are developed through the hymn such that where you end up is a different place from where you have started. This will usually mean that the logic of the words do not work well if you were to repeat parts, or all, of the hymn. Instead, the words take you on a journey from the opening statement to the closing action. Let me give you two examples.

> Come, let us join our cheerful songs
> with angels round the throne;
> ten thousand thousand are their tongues,
> but all their joys are one.
>
> 'Worthy the Lamb that died,' they cry,
> 'to be exalted thus.'
> 'Worthy the Lamb,' our lips reply,
> 'for he was slain for us.'
>
> Jesus is worthy to receive
> honour and power divine;
> and blessings more than we can give,
> be, Lord, for ever thine.
>
> Let all that dwell above the sky,
> and air, and earth, and seas,
> conspire to lift thy glories high,
> and speak thine endless praise
>
> The whole creation join in one,
> to bless the sacred name
> Of him that sits upon the throne,
> and to adore the Lamb.
>
> (Isaac Watts)

First, look at the hymn of Isaac Watts, printed in the box above, which was inspired by Revelation 5.11–13 and was written in the early eighteenth century. As you read through this hymn, you will notice a progression of thought. It begins with an invitation to join the heavenly host in praising God. Evoking the picture of a heavenly throne room from the book of Revelation, it quotes the song of heaven and then invites all creation to join in. It ends with a focus on God and on the ascended Christ, in such a way as to provide a climax of praise focused on God. Of course, you can sing it again, but the logic of the words takes the singer from the invitation to worship, through the heavenly scene, to a vision of all creation praising God. The hymn has a beginning, a middle and an end which means that in worship the internal dynamic can move the congregation on from a gathering for worship to a clear focus on God.

Then take the well-known hymn by Graham Kendrick based on Philippians 2.5–11 (see over). Again, while this hymn is sung to Kendrick's contemporary tune, the form of the piece is still very much a hymn rather than a song. Here again is a progression of thought from the first verse through to the last, although each verse is concluded with a reflective refrain. Verse one is in the form of a prayer addressing Christ and recalling the words of Paul in Philippians chapter two. The refrain offers a reflection, addressed either to the worshipper or to fellow worshippers, a mutual invitation to offer Christ our daily lives of discipleship as an act of worship, recalling Romans 12.1–2. Verse two evokes the garden of Gethsemane and Jesus' struggle to accept the way of the cross, while the next verse invites wonder that the one involved in the creation of the universe should now be subject to death on a cross. The final verse returns to the earlier verse of the Philippians chapter, so that the story of Jesus' descent to earth, and even his submission to an ignominious death for the sake of our salvation, is seen as a model for our own lives of service and forbearance to one another.

Throughout the hymn there is a sense of awe that God should be revealed in humility – remember Wesley's words 'Tis mystery all: the immortal dies!', or even Kendrick's other hymn on this theme, 'Meekness and majesty'. The refrain is a recurring opportunity to respond to the wonderful story of our costly salvation, but the logic of the words is such that it doesn't really make sense to go back to the first verse once you have sung verse four. The hymn takes us on a journey and has the potential to move a congregation forward from reflection on God's love to our consecrated response to that love.

By contrast to this progression of thought through a hymn, the shape of a song lends itself to repetition. A song will tend to have only one

From heaven you came,
  helpless babe,
 entered our world, your glory
  veiled;
not to be served but to serve,
 and give your life that we
  might live.
  *This is our God, the servant*
   *king,*
   *he calls us now to follow*
   *Him,*
  *to bring our lives as a daily*
   *offering*
  *of worship to the servant*
   *king.*

There in the garden of tears,
 my heavy load he chose to
  bear;
his heart with sorrow was torn,
 'Yet not my will but yours,' he
  said.
  *This is our God . . .*

Come see his hands and his
  feet,
 the scars that speak of
  sacrifice;
hands that flung stars into
  space
 to cruel nails surrendered.
  *This is our God . . .*

So let us learn how to serve,
 and in our lives enthrone Him;
each other's needs to prefer,
 for it is Christ we're serving.
  *This is our God . . .*

(Graham Kendrick,
Copyright © 1983 Thankyou Music)

idea, but one which can be impressed on the minds of the singers through repetition. While the linear thought of a hymn lends itself to storytelling, or the development of a theological idea, the simple repetition of a song offers the opportunity for intensification. So our repeating of a basic idea and our response to it has an important part to play in the progression of worship. When we are on a journey we will often see sights which encourage us to pause and appreciate their beauty or grandeur. When faced with a beautiful mountain view, it doesn't make sense to rush on to our next destination, but rather to pause and appreciate what we see. Similarly in worship, we don't undertake the journey always at the same speed, ticking boxes as though we are working through a checklist – praise: done it! confession: done it! responded to God's love: done it! We need to slow down and go deeper. While the linear development of a hymn text may be theologically deeper and richer than a short song, the song enables us to go deeper emotionally as we stay with a theme and engage with it. Sometimes, traditional worshippers complain about what they see as the repetitive nature of worship songs – I have even seen some fold their arms and remain silent when they have sung the lyrics once! This is to confuse the two genres of hymns and songs and to misunderstand the contribution repetitive songs can make to worship.

Again, here are some examples. Brian Doerksen's song on the faithfulness of God is one which is usually repeated when it is used in worship. While there are a number of different thoughts expressed in this song, they all revolve around the worshipper's experience of, and confidence in, God's faithfulness. As the words are repeated, the worshipper is drawn deeper into the remembrance of God's goodness in the past and into an anticipation of, and trust in, God's goodness in the future. This is what I mean by an 'intensification' of the worship moment through repetition, and the cyclic nature of the words enables this to happen.

> Faithful One, so unchanging,
>  Ageless One, you're my rock of
>  peace.
> Lord of all I depend on You,
>  I call out to You, again and
>  again,
>  I call out to You, again and
>  again.
>
> You are my rock in times of
>  trouble
> You lift me up when I fall down.
> All through the storm
> Your love is the anchor;
> My hope is in You alone
>
> (Brian Doerksen,
> Copyright © 1989 Vineyard Songs)

Another example can be seen in Terrye Coelho Strom's simple worship song which can either be sung straight through and then repeated, or sung as a round and repeated. This song is so simple: each verse offers words of adoration and love to the Father, the Son and the Spirit. Thus it evokes the wonder of the triune nature of God revealed in Scripture. We cannot understand or explain this divine richness – but we can adore and respond to God's love with our love. The repetition of the words draws us into the wonder of the life of God and is profoundly theological. The trinity isn't a doctrine that encourages us to list the various 'parts' of God – rather it is an invitation to wonder at the richness of what God has revealed – the diversity

> Father, we adore you,
>  lay our lives before you,
> how we love you.
>
> Jesus, we adore you,
>  lay our lives before you,
> how we love you.
>
> Spirit, we adore you,
>  lay our lives before you,
> how we love you.
>
> (Terrye Coelho Strom,
> Copyright © 1972 Maranatha! Music)

of Father, Son and Spirit and the mutual love in which we are invited to share. The interweaving of song which happens when this is sung as a round is not only musically moving, but by its very shape draws us into the God who is revealed both as one and three. This, again, encourages intensification as we experience something of this richness and respond with adoring love.

Now people could quibble about my structural distinction between hymns and songs as a matter of form and shape, but whether we use the labels of 'hymn' and 'song' in the way I have suggested or not, there is little doubt that a distinction exists. In the next chapter we will see how the difference of form, as well as the content of songs and the mood of the music can all contribute to the planning of worship which is helpful to a congregation.

## Exercise

Choose a few of your favourite hymns and songs, ideally some of each.

Trace the movement in the hymns, as suggested above. Try and put this development of thought through the hymn into your own words.

Identify the main theme in the songs. Try and put into words the effect or impact for a congregation of repeating the song. How might this impact change the more the song is repeated?

# Singing: what and how?

Aim: To explore the potential uses of different kinds of hymns and songs.

Choosing music for worship can be a minefield. Because hymns and songs express and encourage an emotional engagement with the themes of worship, people tend to feel strongly about what they sing.

At one level this can be as simple as people enjoying singing and, in particular, enjoying singing their favourite hymns and songs. Even singing a traditional hymn to the 'wrong' tune has led, at times, to disappointment and complaint! In truth, most hymns were not written to be sung to a particular tune – and different hymnbooks over the years have often set various tunes for the same set of words – but for many people the wedding of words and music has entered deep into their psyche. This doesn't mean that you never choose an alternative tune – but you need to be aware that for some people it can be an issue and you need to do it with your eyes open.

More significant is the expectation, especially for 'occasional' worshippers, that at certain times, such as Christmas and Harvest, their favourite seasonal hymn will be sung. You might wonder whether we should 'pander' to such consumerist expectations. However, if their human disappointment gets in the way of their worshipping we will not have helped them to worship – and if the power of such favourites is so deep-seated then we will need to consider harnessing that power in our worship planning.

## Blended worship

I suspect, however, that sensitivities over hymn tunes are less significant than they used to be and that the provision of predictable favourites may well be seen, not as a negative way of avoiding complaints so much as a positive strategy for encouraging and welcoming people 'back' to church, or for providing a planned 'big moment' in a service. More contentious is the question of worship culture and the great divide that exists in some congregations between the devotees of traditional hymns and the enthusiastic supporters of contemporary worship songs.

My own view is that in the main services of a church, an attempt should be made at what is sometimes called 'blended' worship, an attempt to include a variety of cultural styles in a single worship event. In musical terms this will usually mean including both hymns and songs – playing to their strengths, as we saw in the previous chapter, and using them in a way which not only reaches a range of people who have diverse cultural preferences, but actually stretches worshippers beyond what they personally find comfortable or predictable.

There are two main reasons why blended worship is a good approach to worship planning. First, from a very practical point of view, it makes sense to want to use as broad a range of material as we can in our worship. You would not normally expect an artist to use only two colours when there may be a dozen on their palette. Why should we neglect a whole body of material by ignoring either hymns or songs?

The second main reason for blending our worship is a pastoral, or theological, one and is linked to what we believe about the church. If we believe that the Christian community represents a range of people who might in some ways be quite diverse, but who are reconciled to one another through Christ, and are therefore brothers and sisters in the family of God, then we are going to want ways to worship which both express and encourage this unity in diversity. If reconciliation is at the heart of the gospel, then we want worship which is going to demonstrate this truth.

This doesn't mean that there will not be times when a worship service only uses the resources of a single culture, as staying in that culture may help the worshippers immerse themselves at a deeper level in the dynamics of the service. I call this 'niche' worship – worship for people who 'like that kind of thing' – and it may take the form of a traditional hymn service, a contemporary prayer and praise event, or, for example, a Taizé service of chants and silent meditation. But I believe the main Sunday service of a local congregation should be inclusive in its intent and a blended approach is likely to help this.

## The shape of singing

When we looked at various patterns of services in Chapter 6, we saw that the two most popular in the free churches are what we might call the 'hymn sandwich' and the 'three-decker' service. These are usually associated with the use of hymns or songs respectively, though, in a moment, we shall also look at a blended 'hybrid'.

As we saw in the previous chapter, the internal form of a hymn is quite different from that of a song, and affects how each might be used. Remember that we cannot simply associate hymns with traditional music, and songs with contemporary musical styles. In recent decades, various contemporary tunes have been written for traditional words and, more recently, there has been a trend for contemporary song writers to write new hymns, together with new accompanying music. This is why my basic distinction based on internal form is, I believe, particularly helpful – hymns offer a linear progression of thought, whereas songs tend to be cyclical.

In Figure 1 you can see three varying patterns of singing in worship. In the first example, the hymn sandwich, hymns form the framework, like the bread in a sandwich. The hymns punctuate the worship, providing an opportunity for the congregation to stretch its collective legs, and vocally respond to what has been happening in the service. The first hymn may be a hymn of praise responding to the prompt provided by

| Hymn sandwich | Three-decker service | Blended worship |
|---|---|---|
| Call to Worship | Welcome | Call to Worship |
| **Hymn** | **Song** | **Hymn** |
| Prayer | Scripture verse | Scripture verse |
| **Hymn** | **Song** | **Song** |
| Offering | Brief prayer | Brief prayer |
| Prayer | **Song** | **Song** |
| **Hymn** | **Song** | Offering |
| Reading | Silence | Prayers |
| Sermon | Offering | Reading |
| **Hymn** | **Song** | Sermon |
| Blessing | Sermon | **Hymn** |
| | Prayer | Brief prayer |
| | **Song** | **Song** |
| | Ministry time | Blessing |
| | Closing prayer | |

**Figure 1**

the call to worship. The second hymn may be a prayerful link between prayers of confession and thanksgiving and wider intercessory prayers for the world. The hymn before the sermon may be one proclaiming our salvation and God's goodness, or it may be one which affirms God's word or asks for the help of the Holy Spirit as we seek the mind of Christ in Scripture. The hymn after the sermon will probably be a hymn which enables the congregation to respond to the invitation or challenge of the sermon. It may be a prayer of dedication or a looking forward in faith to what God's goodness will reveal in the days ahead.

When selecting hymns in this kind of service it will be very important to look at what is happening immediately before and after each hymn. Because the hymn provides a progression of thought through its verses, the worship planner will want to ensure that the hymn takes people from one point to the next in the journey of worship.

In the three-decker service the songs operate differently. Instead of being interspersed at intervals through the service, they provide most of the meat as well as the bread in the sandwich! Usually they will be planned in a block early in the service. As we saw in Chapter 6, this is often called 'a time of worship' which isn't very helpful as it implies that the rest of the service isn't. Of course, what is meant is that 'worship' means a close encounter with God, and the songs are believed to help people focus emotionally as well as mentally on God in an intense and sustained way. Sometimes there will be no link between one song and the next, but a continuum of singing. Sometimes there will be brief prayers which focus the sentiment of the singing or Scripture verses which prompt the next song.

In this kind of service, the movement happens in the transition from one song to the next, rather than within the songs. The repetition of a song intensifies the worship moment rather than progresses it, so the worship planner will want to choose those moments which are most helpfully intensified. Also, when there is a block of songs the journey of the service will need to happen within that block of singing. This will mean that praise, confession and thanksgiving, for example, will need to be enabled by the choice of songs and the manner of their links.

In a blended service the opportunity for both these approaches becomes available. Hymns can lead us forward through the progression of their verses, or a song can hold us in a moment of powerful focus and intensity. What is important is that we choose what will be helpful to a particular congregation and that we are familiar with the characteristics and opportunities of each genre in order to use each most effectively.

# What shall we sing?

It ought to be clear by now that I don't commend the approach which simply chooses the worship leader's favourite hymns or songs. That would soon get very boring, and would not enable the kind of worship planning which this book has been trying to encourage.

Of course, there is a question as to who chooses the hymns and songs. In many churches this will simply be the minister or person leading the service. Sometimes, however, especially in churches which use the three-decker approach, the block of singing will be led by a musician, and it may be that person who selects the songs. If that is the case, then it is important that there is a discussion with the lead musician about the theme of the service and what you hope will be its journey from gathering to sending. We cannot assume that, simply because someone can sing or play the guitar, that they are gifted in leading worship, but it is important that we work sensitively with whoever else is entrusted by the church with sharing in the leading of worship. In the longer term, if this partnership is going to be a continuing one then you might like to give the musician a copy of this book!

But for now, let's assume that you are selecting the hymns and songs, albeit consulting with others as appropriate. So how do we go about the business of selection? There are some general questions and specific questions which are going to help us. The general questions might include:

1  **What is the culture of the congregation?**
   It is important to know what will come easily to the congregation and what will be more difficult. Do they normally sing hymns? Do they know many songs? Are they used to standing for a sustained period? And so on.

2  **What are the available musical resources?**
   Do we have a musician who can play syncopated music? Do we only have an organ? Or even, do we have any musicians at all? These practical considerations are important, for, however well planned the service is, if it doesn't work at the basic level of people being able to sing what has been selected, then the worship will be in trouble.

3  **What time of year is it?**
   We will look at the seasons of the Christian year in Chapter 17. But, for now, we need to recognize that if it is Advent or Christmas, or Holy Week or Easter or Pentecost, then we will need to choose at least

some of the hymns and songs which are normally associated with these seasons. Again, this is about practicalities – both the expectation of the congregation and the capacity of particular hymns and songs to connect with the gospel truths which each season celebrates.

The more specific questions are ones we might ask of a particular hymn or song and might be summarized as, 'Does this fit here?' These questions might include:

1 **What worship action is the song enabling?**
   In other words, what place does the hymn or song have in the service? Is it praise, or thanksgiving, or personal dedication, or what? This is a vital question in any selection process.

2 **What happens before and after?**
   What prompts the song and what will happen next after it? Will you choose a song which intensifies a moment, or a hymn which will lead you from one point of focus to another?

3 **What mood will be most helpfully evoked?**
   Is it a time for celebration, or reflective quiet, for up-beat involvement or plaintive lamenting?

4 **Are there Scripture references which we want the hymn or song to echo?**
   We may link 'The Servant King' with Philippians 2 or the story of Jesus washing the feet of the disciples. We may link, for example, the song 'Lord, I come to you', with its words 'and as I wait, I'll rise up like the eagle' with Isaiah 40.31, to which it refers, or to some other Scripture passage about the faithfulness and grace of God.

5 **Do we know it?**
   This may seem an obvious question but it is important to ask it. If a congregation is singing something for the first time, or is not very familiar with the tune, then it will not help people as much as it might because they will be focusing on getting the tune right, or fitting the words to the tune, rather than using the song as a vehicle for worship. This doesn't mean, of course, that we never choose new songs or hymns. But it does mean that we are careful where they come in a service – probably not a crucial moment – and probably not more than one new song in any service.

---

**Exercise**

Plan a service in each of the three shapes illustrated in Figure 1. Use the same theme for each so you can explore the relative opportunities which each service shape provides. Possible themes might include: creation, forgiveness, or serving others.

---

## Getting organized

If you are involved in leading worship regularly in the same congregation, then it will be very important that you bring some organization to your selection of hymns and songs. For example, it will be important not to flog a song to death. However good it might be, and however much the congregation appreciate it, if you sing something too often then it is likely to lose its power to help people worship. When a congregation learns a new song it may be helpful to have it several times in the course of the next few weeks, but it will then be important to make sure that afterwards it is chosen when it is the 'right' choice for a particular point in a particular service – rather than simply because the worship leader likes it or the congregation is still getting a buzz over it.

It will therefore be helpful if you keep a record of what you sing on what date. I do this by filing my orders of service on my computer. I am not constantly looking back to see what we sang and when, but if I sense that I might be choosing something too soon after having sung it previously, then it is an easy matter to go back through the orders of service for the previous few weeks.

It is also helpful to have a good list of hymns and songs from which to choose. The index of a hymn book may be very helpful, as will the lists which some books include which enumerate the hymns and songs which are relevant to particular themes. Now that many churches are increasingly using different sources for their singing material, it is helpful if you can have an easy way of accessing all the available material which the congregation knows or might sing. This will widen your choice and help you to choose hymns and songs appropriate for particular places in particular services.

## Screens, books and copyright

Increasing numbers of churches no longer place hymnbooks in the hands of the congregation. Either they are printing the words of hymns and songs on a service leaflet, or projecting them by means of an overhead projector or, more commonly, by a data projector linked to a laptop. There are various advantages to this, not least the wider selection of hymns and songs which becomes available. It is also strongly argued by some that the change from looking down at a book to looking up at a screen improves the quality of the singing, as well as leaving hands free for praise movements.

However, if you are printing the words of modern hymns and songs you must remember and respect the fact that they will be protected by copyright laws. This is usually no great burden. There is a copyright licensing scheme available (see the resources section at the end of the book) which enables a church to pay an annual fee and use free of charge all the songs which are covered by the licence. Be careful, however, as not all publishers participate in the scheme, and you may need to seek permission to use occasional hymns or songs. This whole process has been simplified in recent years by the use of song software available for church computers. The software usually provides a presentation system which offers ready designs for songs and other worship material to be projected. The software usually includes a huge list of songs and hymns, all of which have copyright permission for use with the software programme. If you print or project copyright material you need to keep a list of what you have used, so this requirement can be combined with a list of available songs and hymns as well as keeping track of how often the congregation sings them.

You might think that all this is very complicated – that's because it is! But if you note a number of basic principles then you can organize your own system for selecting hymns and songs as long as you do so legally and creatively, so as to enable the congregation to worship God worthily. Now might be the time to think about how you can better organize your own system of selecting hymns and songs.

---

### Exercise

Make a list of all the hymns and songs which are sung at your church over the next four weeks. What are the dominant themes conveyed by these hymns and songs? Are there important themes which have not been covered at all?

---

# 12

# Living with Scripture

> Aim: To understand why Scripture should be a central feature of worship, both as God's word addressed to the congregation and as God-given words to help our worship of God.

What makes Christian worship Christian? We have already seen that one answer to this question is to say that Christians gather for worship 'in the name of Jesus'. This doesn't only mean that they end their prayers with words such as 'through Jesus Christ our Lord', but that the worship event and the attitudes and hopes of the congregation are 'in the spirit of Jesus', or in line with the character of Jesus.

But how does this work in practice? How do we know what the character of Jesus is like? Of course, all we know about Jesus we have learned from our reading of the Bible – and all we believe about God is based on what we read in the Bible concerning his dealings with the world. Christians speak of the Bible as 'the word of God', though they will interpret that phrase in a variety of ways.

## The word of God

I believe that the Bible is the inspired 'word of God'. This is true in more than one way and I think that our appreciation of this will help our leading of, and participation in, worship. Through the Bible, God speaks to us today, but the work of the Holy Spirit in that exciting prospect is a dynamic one, both in the past and the present.

1  God was at work in the events of history which are reported in Scripture. God called Abraham, freed the Hebrew slaves, came among us in the birth and life of Jesus, raised him from the dead and guided the early Church in its mission to the world. This was God working in the world and so was the activity of the Holy Spirit: God's power and presence at work.

2  God was at work inspiring the writers of the biblical books to testify to what God had done and to their own experience of God at work in their lives and situations. I think that God respected their freedom as human beings in this process – he did not dictate to secretaries, or treat them as human typewriters. They needed to exercise faith to hear his word to them and to pass that word on through story-telling, history, Law, prophecy and so on. The Holy Spirit inspired the gospel writers to put in writing the incidents they had witnessed or the stories of Jesus they had heard.

3  The Holy Spirit inspired the leaders of Israel, and then the leaders of the early Church to recognize certain writings as 'Scripture', or God's word to us. The Bible is the Church's book, not only in the sense that it should be the foundation of the Church's teaching and practice, but it is the book which the Holy Spirit inspired the Church to compile and recognize and receive as 'God's word'.

4  Finally, Scripture is God's word today, or, rather, the means by which God speaks to us today. As we read Scripture, the Holy Spirit inspires us anew to hear whatever it is that God seeks to say to us. This is a dynamic process which needs faith, humility and creative imagination.

This dynamic picture has at least two implications which I think are important in our preparation for, and involvement in, worship. First, it offers us an exciting way of understanding our relationship to the word of God. It reminds us that in all our Christian understanding we are dependent on God. God's word is not frozen in time, to be dissected with the scalpel of human skill and knowledge and placed on a slab for the inspection of the congregation! God's word is alive as we read and preach and listen. The Holy Spirit warms our hearts, clears our minds and quickens our imaginations.

Yet this (truly) inspirational activity is not a free-wheeling flight of fancy, where we can believe whatever we want to believe, or say whatever we want to say. This inspiring work of the Spirit happens through our reading of Scripture and is consistent with what God has already revealed of his purposes and character. To mix our metaphors, Scripture both provides the raw materials which the Spirit uses to speak afresh to us, and offers the anchor which keeps our receiving of the living word in our contemporary situation firmly in line with what he has already revealed. In John's Gospel, Jesus tells the disciples of the coming of the Holy Spirit:

> When the Spirit of truth comes, he will guide you into all truth; for he will not speak on his own, but will speak whatever he hears, and he will declare to you the things that are to come. He will glorify me, because he will take what is mine and declare it to you.
>
> (John 16.13–14)

Second, we need to recognize another dimension to the work of the Holy Spirit in our reading of Scripture. The preacher will come to a view as to what is the central message of the Scripture reading for the congregation, and will seek to communicate that in an interesting and lively manner. But God may also be speaking to individual members of the congregation – sometimes applying to their hearts what the preacher is saying, and sometimes applying something quite distinct from it. This is the sovereign work of the Spirit at work in the congregation. Just as the congregation prays as a community and as a collection of individual persons, so God may address the congregation as a community and at the same time address individuals in their specific needs and circumstances. Is this not awesome?

In the first part of this section, I have written of how we can understand the inspiration of Scripture as a multiple and dynamic reality. But there is another way in which we can explore this multiple reality. I have said that Scripture is the 'inspired word of God' and have examined what I mean by 'inspired'. But we can also trace multiple meanings in the phrase 'word of God'. Again, I don't want to begin with Scripture but with the activity of God.

Jesus Christ is the Word of God. The opening chapter of John's Gospel presents us with a vision of the eternal Word, God's self-communication with all that has been created. The Gospel then identifies this wonderful reality with the specific person of Jesus: 'And the Word became flesh and lived among us, and we have seen his glory, the glory of a father's only son, full of grace and truth' (John 1.14). This is vitally important: God's central and fullest revelation of his will is Jesus Christ, God's word made flesh, and all our claims of what God might be saying to us or through us need to be tested by what Scripture tells us of Jesus.

Of course, we only know about Jesus through Scripture. Here are the stories and the teaching, and here is the impact of Jesus on the lives of the first Christians. The Old Testament presents God as the gracious and merciful creator, and seeks fellowship with a runaway and sinful world. It prepares us for the coming of Jesus who spoke both about 'fulfilling' the law and the prophets and yet also of superseding them: 'You have heard that it was said, "An eye for an eye and a tooth for a tooth." But I say to you, Do not resist an evildoer. But if anyone strikes you on the right cheek, turn the other also' (Matthew 5.17, 38–39).

Scripture is the word of God in the sense that it bears witness to the Word of God: Jesus Christ. And we should always read Scripture in the light of Jesus and what has been revealed to us in and through him. He becomes the interpretative key that helps us to understand, the acid test that ensures we haven't got the wrong end of the stick. We need to take to heart his rebuke of the religious authorities of his day: 'You search the scriptures because you think that in them you have eternal life; and it is they that testify on my behalf. Yet you refuse to come to me to have life' (John 5.39–40). The words of Scripture point to Jesus, and it is he who is Lord of the church, not a book, however holy.

This is why, when the church gathers for worship, it both gathers in the name of Jesus and gathers around God's word. Scripture should have a central place in our worship, for it is in and through Scripture that God speaks to us afresh the word of forgiveness and hope which is fully revealed and effected in Jesus Christ.

## God's word to us: Scripture as revelation

So in the planning of worship, how are we to arrange things so that we can hear God speak to us through Scripture? The most obvious and most important is that we read passages of Scripture as part of the worship event. This was a central feature of worship in the synagogues of Jesus' day and has been a key feature of Christian worship from the beginning.

It is important that Scripture speaks for itself. It should be read aloud and have its own place in the service. Perhaps this is a good opportunity to make a plea that there should always be at least one Bible reading. Sometimes, preachers just read a verse or two of Scripture and preach on that. The danger is that these verses are simply a peg on which to hang the preacher's thoughts. The sermon should normally be an exposition of the Bible reading, and it is important that preachers are subject to the reading, rather than manipulate the reading by making it fit what they want to say. Of course, the reading will often be selected with a view to preaching on a particular subject, but a Bible reading of more than a couple of verses will enable the congregation to hear more easily the voice of Scripture and not just the voice of the preacher.

There are, of course, practical considerations. How many readings should there be? Some churches have three (Old Testament, Epistle and Gospel) while others think that one is sufficient. It is a good rule of thumb that you should usually have somewhere between ten and twenty-five verses of Scripture read aloud and that, if there is more than one reading they should be connected in some thematic way which will make sense to, rather than distract, the congregation. Less than (very roughly) ten verses could easily be taken out of context and over twenty-five will be more than some congregations can cope with. Local culture is important here. Some will encourage people

> ### Exercise
>
> Your church has decided to have a six week series on the Parables of Jesus.
>
> Choose six parables which you think would go well together in a series. Then choose an Old Testament passage for each parable which you feel would be good to read as well as the parable in the services.

to follow the reading in their own Bibles, or Bibles that are provided, or with the biblical words on a screen. This may well help concentration. Others prefer the congregation to listen, rather than read along, as, they argue, Scripture was originally written to be read aloud and heard. They argue that reading creates a 'study mentality', where we dissect Scripture, rather than a frame of mind that is creatively open to the Spirit touching our imaginations. The choice is yours!

How do we select the Bible readings? Some churches will follow a lectionary, or plan of Bible readings, through the year. The most commonly used work on a three-year cycle which observes the major Christian festivals. We shall look at this in more detail in the chapter on the Christian year. For now, we may simply observe that this is one means of selection – following an ecumenically agreed scheme of readings Sunday by Sunday. Other churches may well have their own, locally devised, plan of readings, often in the form of sermon series, where books of the Bible are expounded over a period of weeks.

If someone is asked to lead a service in a church which follows one of these plans, they may be asked to fit in with the programme. Alternatively, someone may be given a free hand and told something like, 'Bring the word which God lays on your heart for us.' The preacher needs to prayerfully consider the circumstance of the congregation and think about what might be the 'right' theme and the 'right' reading for that circumstance. If you find that you are getting nowhere slowly, you might consider reflecting on what God is saying to you at that time – it may be that the word which excites you personally is what God wants you to share with others. But remember, it must be based on your reading of Scripture and be tested in the light of Jesus Christ.

How might the Bible readings happen? They are a good opportunity to involve someone else in sharing in the leading of worship, and some churches will have rotas of people who read week by week. Another voice from the front is healthy, and the more people who participate in this way, the more the worship is able to express the communal nature of the church. If there is more than one reading, then ask more than one reader. Sometimes, it might be helpful to have a dramatized reading where a Bible story is read by a number of different people taking the part of different characters in the reading. Sometimes you may want to read at least part of the reading more than once in the service – perhaps at the end of the sermon, or as a prompt for reflective prayers.

Remember God addresses us through Scripture, and its reading should be full of promise and dramatic tension: it should be listened to with anticipation and hope. The worship leader should try and encourage this to happen.

---

### Exercise

Make a short survey of the Bible readings at your church for the next few weeks, noting what passages were read, how long they were and who read them. Add alongside this information your own reaction and reflections: were the passages appropriate, too long, too short or the right length, and read well?

How might this exercise help you as you prepare to lead worship? Might it change the way you do things sometimes?

---

## Our words to God: Scripture as worship

While the primary place of Scripture in worship is as God's word to us, there has been a long tradition of Christians using the words of Scripture as a way of offering worship to God. Indeed, many of those biblical words were first written as words for worship. The book of Psalms is the obvious example, where we find both personal and communal examples of prayer to God. There are also passages in the New Testament which have long been used in worship, such as the Magnificat, or Mary's Song (Luke 1.46–55), or the Nunc Dimittis, or the Song of Simeon (Luke 2.29–32). In addition, there are passages of Scripture which might well have originated as words for worship before they were incorporated by the biblical writers. Examples are the song of the servant king (Philippians 2.6–11) and the snatches of heavenly worship in Revelation chapters four and five. These will often offer helpful words for a congregation to use in its own worship and many have been incorporated into hymns and songs at different times.

There are three main ways in which biblical words might be used in our worship of God. First, through the intentional use of such words as a way of expressing the concerns of the congregation or prompting appropriate sentiments on the part of the congregation. In this way, the reading of Scripture is used as stepping stones in the service, rather than as the main event. Here are some of the most likely forms this will take:

- **Call to worship** – At the beginning of the service, the worship leader might read a verse or a few verses of Scripture which express some truth about God's character or saving action. This call to worship focuses the attention of the gathering congregation on God and has the additional purpose of prompting the first expressions of praise on the part of the congregation. It is important to ensure a link between such a call to worship and the words of the opening hymn or song, which might be an echo of the call. Lamentations 3.22–23 could, for example, be followed by 'Great is thy faithfulness', a hymn based on those verses. Alternatively, it might be a hymn which responds to the promise or declaration of the call: Isaiah 40.28–31 could be followed by 'Praise to the Lord, the Almighty, the king of creation', which emphasizes the greatness and compassion of God, or 'Lord, I come to you' which picks up the theme of God's raising us up from our weakness and need, and echoes the reference to soaring like an eagle.
- **Worship links** – Just as a call to worship starts things off, so a link verse can connect one part of a service with another. A sequence of songs, for example, might be joined by brief prayers or a Scripture verse. Sometimes such a verse might lead into a moment of silent reflection before continuing with a prayer or a song.
- **Prayer prompt** – Sometimes a Scripture verse will provide the starting point for a prayer, or a longer passage may provide the framework for a meditation or a series of requests.

The second way in which Scripture provides the congregation with words for the worship of God is by the use of quotations in prayers, hymns and songs. It has always been a common practice of worship to quote Scripture as a means of expressing something we believe deeply. Hymns are often full of scriptural phrases. Indeed sometimes they are wholly paraphrases of scriptural passages. 'The Lord's my shepherd' is, of course, a paraphrase of Psalm 23 and 'All people that on earth do dwell' is a paraphrase of Psalm 100. Many contemporary worship songs are paraphrases of biblical words, or the development of biblical ideas.

Finally, there is the congregational reading of Scripture. Usually, this will be arranged as a responsive reading, with the leader and the congregation alternating, or two sides of the congregation reading antiphonally – that is where one section of the congregation reads a line, and another section responds with the next line, and so on. It is important that you don't just use the verse divisions, as sometimes they are quite arbitrary (and not original to the Bible). Instead, try to script the voice divisions so that the two or more voices illuminate the meaning of the words. Give the congregation a voice – and what better script than the word of God, which we offer back as our words.

---

### Exercise

Prepare a Bible reading for congregational use:

- Select the Bible reading so that it makes sense as words addressed to God or a mixture of words addressed to one another, or to ourselves and to God.
- Write these words out in your word processor or, better still, copy them from a Bible software package and paste them into your word processor.
- Read though the words a couple of times and work out if there are different 'voices' present. Will some verses make a response, or will some act as a prompt for what comes next?
- Put into bold type the words which you think most appropriate for the congregation to say. Here is a clue: give them the 'best' or most declaratory words. Let the leader's words be a cue for the main words which are to be said by the congregation.
- Print the result in a congregational leaflet, OHP acetate or in a software programme suitable for a data projector.

# 13

# Plotting the preaching

> Aim: To understand the purpose of preaching
> and some of the varied ways in which God's
> word can be communicated.

If you have been asked to lead worship this may include an invitation to preach, or it may not. Leading worship and preaching do not necessarily need the same gifts, though often people who do the one will do the other! Because this may be something you are called to do, we shall spend some time looking at the basic principles in this chapter, and some practical guidelines for making a start in preaching in the next.

It has been said that the age of preaching is over, yet still people are called to help congregations make connections between Christian Scripture and their daily living as Christians. Traditionally this has been in the form of an address presented by one person to the congregation, and we call it a 'sermon'. Although there are other ways of communicating ideas, such as through drama or discussion, we shall concentrate here on the traditional 'sermon', though we shall note some recent innovations in the way preaching is understood and practised.

But what of the claim that the sermon is dead? There are a number of cultural factors which have led some critics to make such a judgement:

- Changes in social attitudes have made people far less deferential to authority figures than in previous times. This means that the preacher cannot start from an assumption that people will simply accept what a preacher says, just because they are the preacher. I suspect that this never was the case, but the age of deference is over and that presents the preacher with a challenging context in which to work.

- There have been changing expectations in how people communicate. We live in a visual age in which people have little tolerance for 'talking heads' and have a short concentration span. The preacher can't ignore this.
- Educational insights have led us to see that people learn best through participation, 'hands-on' experimentation and learning from life, and a monologue is not the most effective way of communicating truth. This may be true, but people have different learning styles and we have to ask whether preaching is primarily about teaching and learning, or something else.

You will probably gather from my comments after each point that I see these challenges as just that – challenges which affect how we set about preaching, rather than a death sentence on preaching itself. The reality is that congregations need to listen to Scripture and need help in listening for God's voice addressing their situation. While small congregations may be able to engage in discussion, this isn't going to work for larger gatherings and, anyway, I believe there is still an important role for passionate, personal communication. We need to recognize the communication issues, and we need to learn from what we might call 'best practice', but there is still a job to be done, and God still calls people to preach and congregations to listen! So let's look at some of the principles.

## By whose authority?

So most services will still have a sermon or a time when the leader is able to address the congregation. This is not an opportunity for the preacher to share his or her own views on life in general, politics, morality or even Christian belief. It is an opportunity for the preacher to speak on behalf of God.

'Who do they think they are?' might be a natural response to such a claim, and 'I could never claim to speak on behalf of God' might be an understandable reaction. Yet here are some things for you to think about:

- God normally communicates with people through other people.
- God has communicated with us through the Bible and, especially, through Jesus Christ.

- Someone needs to make the connection between the world of the Bible and the world in which the worshippers live.
- People don't preach because they fancy it as a pastime or because they want to show off, but because some part of the church has recognized God-given gifts and has entrusted them with the business of trying to understand and communicate some aspect of God's will for a particular situation.

As you are reading this book, it is likely that other people have recognized something in you which they believe can be developed. Most times when someone preaches it is because they have been invited to do so, or they have been appointed to a role in the church, of which preaching is a part. So what's it all about?

## Bible-centred worship and Christ-centred living

Christians are called to live their lives in fellowship with Jesus Christ. Christian living is Christ-centred living and one of the main ways we sustain this is through gathering with other Christians for worship.

A key way of ensuring that worship will sustain healthy Christian living is by making sure that the Bible is a central feature of worship. We have already seen how the Bible is a resource for songs and prayers, but it has an even more obvious and crucial role. Each service of Christian worship should contain at least one reading from the Bible. This is 'God's word', and if we are to remain faithful in our lives we need to be receptive to what God has said through Scripture and what God continues to say through our own reading of Scripture, with the guidance of the Holy Spirit. We listen to God's word and we respond both in worship and in our daily living – which is also our worship.

This is why we preach. The sermon is an attempt, with God's help and our hard work, to make connections between what God has already inspired people to write in Scripture and what God wants to communicate to the followers of Jesus today. This process will involve the preacher in a variety of things – prayerful reflection, Bible study, sympathetic imagination in an at-

> **Exercise**
>
> Why preach? Write in one sentence what *you think* the answer should be.

tempt to understand the congregation – and a commitment to communicating clearly and persuasively.

## Communicating good news

One of the leading contemporary writers on preaching, Fred Craddock, has said that in preparing a sermon a preacher has to make two key deci- sions – what to say and how to say it. He goes on to comment that most preachers seem to spend most of their preparation time on the first task – deciding what to say – and not enough time on the second – choosing the best way to say it.

Ever since the time of the early Church, preachers have recognized that communicating clearly and persuasively is a skill which some people may have naturally, but which all would be wise to develop conscientiously. The preacher needs to build a rapport with the congregation, and this will usually be achieved in the early part of the sermon. It will strengthen the preacher's credibility and will help the congregation to take seriously the reasoned arguments of the sermon and any impassioned appeal which may accompany them.

Preaching is partly about communicating information, particularly from the Bible, and from the wisdom of Christians who have gone before us. But it is also about persuasion. We need to persuade people to be encouraged, or to be challenged, to trust God more, or to see the world through God's eyes. We should not try to manipulate people, but we should help them to see the good news of God's love in the light of the Bible reading which the sermon explores.

## Personal styles and varied forms

The shape and style of sermons can vary enormously. If the sermon is a genuine attempt to communicate the meaning of a Bible passage or verse, then it is reasonable that the style of the biblical material will affect the style of the sermon. The Bible contains a wide variety of material – his- tory, poetry, proverbs, law, stories, letters, and so on. It is not a good idea to think that only one kind of sermon will communicate the truths contained in this rich diversity.

Yet often, when people begin to preach, they think that there is only one 'right' way of writing a sermon. Of course, what they envisage that 'best' way to be will vary according to their church tradition and back- ground. They may envisage an expository sermon with an introduction, three points and a conclusion; or they may think of an informal, conver- sational address which begins with a couple of jokes, strings together a couple of biblical observations and a series of stories and ends with an appeal. They may imagine a brief homily which dare not be more than ten minutes and which tries to avoid challenging the congregation too much!

These examples may be a bit of a caricature – but only a bit! It can be both limiting and even dangerous to think that there is only one way to preach. The diversity of Scripture, the diversity of personality among preachers, and the diversity of congregations, all demand that we don't stick to one kind of sermon. This is why, in recent years, there has been a growing interest in the range of styles open to the preacher. A few examples are shown in Figure 1.

| Different Types of Preaching | |
|---|---|
| Expository preaching | For many evangelical churches this may be regarded as a kind of default position. Yet it can itself take a variety of forms: if a passage of Scripture is the subject, then it may be shaped as a verse-by-verse commentary (though there needs to be the unity of a main point to the sermon). Alternatively, it may be a number of key points which un-pack a single verse. Whichever form is used, expository preaching is likely to major on explaining and applying the biblical text. |
| Narrative preaching | As its name suggests, narrative preaching is communi-cation through story telling. It may involve the re-telling of a Bible story (such as a monologue from one of the characters in a story) or it may be a modern parable which expresses the main point you want to communicate from the Bible reading. Importantly, this method will usually leave the congregation to make the connections, while the preacher just tells a story! |
| Topical preaching | This is where the starting point and aim of the sermon is to address some contemporary issue in the public arena, or matters of concern to individuals in the congregation. This is still biblical preaching because the discussion of the topic involves Christian response which is authorita-tively informed by a Christian reading of Scripture. |
| Doctrinal preaching | This is similar to topical preaching, but the main theme expounds an aspect of Christian belief. It may relate to a specific Bible reading, or it may draw on different parts of Scripture. However, it is important that a doctrine not only be explained, but that its significance for Christian living be explored and applied. |

| Prophetic preaching | Prophetic preaching may begin with an exposition of one of the biblical prophets, such as Isaiah or Hosea, or it may aim to interpret contemporary events in a way which applies biblical truth. It has been said that the preacher should prepare with the Bible in one hand and the newspaper in the other. This is particularly true for prophetic preaching, as the signs of the times become a key focus. Yet it still remains vital that such preaching is not an opportunity for the preacher to communicate political preferences to the congregation, but is a genuine attempt to make connections between Scripture and daily life. |
|---|---|
| Devotional preaching | This preaching has at its heart a concern to help the members of the congregation open themselves to God working in their lives. This may begin with the exposition of a psalm, or some other biblical material, or it may begin with 'problems' in the Christian life, such as difficulties in prayer. It may be more reflective in mood and should always be encouraging and full of the love and grace of God. |
| Meditation | Sometimes a service calls for a short, reflective piece in which the preacher 'thinks aloud', and encourages thoughtful meditation upon Scripture, some aspect of God's love or each person's place on the journey of faith. |
| Evangelistic preaching | From time to time the Christian faith will be presented in such a way as to encourage people to turn to Christ and put their faith in him for the first time. This is always likely to be in the context of a congregation where many are already believers, so evangelistic preaching in worship ought to include in the challenge an opportunity for believers to renew their commitment to Christ as well an invitation for those who may come to faith for the first time. |
| **Figure 1** | |

---

### Exercise

Read these different passages from the Bible: Genesis 12.1–9; Deuteronomy 16.1–15; Psalm 51; Isaiah 40.1–11; Luke 14.12–24; Romans 12.1–21.

Starting with the passage itself and the way that it presents ideas, what type of sermon, from the list above, do you think might be appropriate for each of the different passages?

Try sketching out, and even preaching, a sermon in a type different to your normal style (if you have one!)

---

## Structure or movement?

Recent thinking on preaching has also led to quite a change in the way sermon preparation and delivery have been viewed. In particular, attention has been drawn to the oral and aural nature of preaching. In other words preaching is spoken and heard – not written and read! The way we communicate in speaking to people is different from how we communicate in writing. When we speak we need to ensure clarity through simplicity, and often through repetition. If I read something and I don't understand it the first time, I can go back and read it again. This can't happen when I am listening to someone – unless it's a recording which I can rewind! So preaching as an oral medium means I have to speak clearly and simply, ensuring that when I move from one point to another, people are going with me and are not still wondering what I meant a few minutes ago.

One writer, Eugene Lowry, has spoken of seeing the sermon as an 'event-in-time'. This means that we recognize that the linear nature of the spoken word requires us to

---

### Exercise

Read a copy of a sermon you have written (ideally in full script) alongside a newspaper item, a church magazine article, or a report from a charity. Note down the different ways words and sentences are used.

Ask your minister or another experienced preacher if you can borrow a sermon script from them and compare this with other pieces of writing.

---

take people on a journey. The way we prepare and the way we present needs to acknowledge this dynamic relationship between speaker and hearers.

Textbooks used to speak of 'sermon construction', where the preacher prepared an outline which was seen as a kind of scaffolding around which the sermon was built point by point, or brick by brick. However, this is now seen by many as too static – it's suitable for writing something which people will read, like this book, but not for something which people will hear.

So preaching is an oral medium in that we speak it – and an aural medium in that others will hear it. The preacher has to lead us through a train of thought which we can follow easily – while still maintaining our interest with an element of suspense and surprise. As a result, instead of using a building-site image of sermon constructing, we can use the cinematic image of plotting a story line for a film. What matters is not so much the component parts of the sermon, as the progression of thought, the movement through which the congregation is led to see something new in the Bible passage and face up to what God might be saying to them through it. This is a dynamic way of preparing a sermon, and one which may liberate us to take more seriously the different styles and biblical material available.

However, make sure that your sermon has one main theme or point and don't try to say too many different things. People will not easily remember a number of points – even when they all start with the same letter! Have one main aim, though it may be applied in a number of different ways to different types of hearer. That aim should be a positive one and should relate to something we believe about God. This will help you organize your material more effectively, it should lead to more impact in delivery and it should help you to prepare the worship – especially those parts which will follow the sermon. But more of this in the next chapter.

---

### Exercise

Now re-read the six passages listed in the previous exercise but one and work out what you think the one main theme for a sermon on this passage might be. Try and write the main point in one sentence for each of the passages.

---

# 14

# Starting the sermon

> Aim: To explore some basic strategies for preparing a sermon.

Theory is all very well, but what about the practicalities? How do I decide what to say? How do I plan how I'm going to say it? How long should I preach? Should I do it 'off the cuff', or should I have a full, written script? And what about illustrations or jokes? Help! Well, here are some guidelines. Treat them as just that, not as unchangeable rules. And after each time you have preached, reflect on whether the method you used has worked and ask yourself if you should do anything differently next time.

## Script, prompt or what?

When you are a beginning to preach, it is probably a good idea to write out a full script as part of your preparation. Some gifted and experienced preachers will use such a script when they preach – others will try to memorize it – while others will shorten it to a series of prompts which help them to repeat the gist of their full script, with the important bits perhaps written in full.

Remember, the important thing is to communicate clearly. If you are reading from a full script, you should know it well enough to be able to look at the congregation from time to time – especially for those sentences which challenge or inspire. If you are working with notes or prompts, then you need to be sufficiently conversant with your material that you will not hesitate too much or be lost for words. Again, remember that preaching is interpersonal – you are speaking to people, not making announcements in front of them! The way you support your memory in preaching needs to take account of that, as well as providing you with the things you need to say.

## How long is a piece of string?

Beginners can get hung up on length. Obviously, a sermon needs to be long enough to cover what needs to be said – but it also needs to be short enough to be interesting. It's of no use if you make all the points you believe need to be made in a sermon, yet lose the congregation part way through.

Local custom and expectation will provide a context in which the preacher works, and we should respect that culture. One congregation will expect ten minutes, while another will assume fifty minutes and, perhaps most anticipate around twenty. Most should be tolerant of a beginner – provided the beginner doesn't go on too long. Better too short than too long – so relax about those anxieties that you will dry up and appear a stammering wreck. Just make sure you have worked on the closing section of your sermon and know it well – far better to jump to your closing words because you have nothing more to say in the middle, than to go on endlessly because you haven't worked carefully on your finish!

## United we stand

Yes, I said this in the last chapter but it's so important I'm going to say it again! Aim for one main point in your sermon. Until you are more experienced, it will be a good practice for you to write down what you believe the aim of the sermon is going to be. Write it down after your initial work, but before you write a detailed script or the notes you will use in your delivery.

**One main point:**
- will be remembered
- will communicate clearly
- will enable you to organize your material around it and in support of it
- will enable you to provide a thematic focus for the worship service

**Figure 1**

One main point is enough – two is too many. In Figure 1 you can see some of the reasons why one aim is enough and in fact how it will help you communicate more effectively. It will help you plan and it will help you be more punchy in your delivery. Don't worry if you don't seem to have enough material. There is no point having more material if it is off the point! Focus – a clear aim – that's your best strategy for effective communication.

## What and how

Remember Fred Craddock's observation that there are two tasks for the person preparing to preach. First you decide what you need to say (in other words, your main theme or the aim of the sermon) and then, second, you work out how best to say it. His comment that many preachers don't seem to move on to this second stage is salutary.

How can I best communicate this theme to this congregation? The answer will vary according to your own strengths and the characteristics of the particular congregation. To separate out these two stages of preparation – what and how – should remind you that it is very important to ask about your method of communication. What kind of sermon? What style of preaching? What thought progression will engage the listeners and help them to see the point you are trying to communicate?

## Mapping the sermon

One way in which you can distinguish between the content of the sermon and the way in which you are going to communicate that content, is to map the sermon. Before I explain how to do this, let me give you an illustration. Let's suppose you put ten household objects on a table. Then you group them according to size, or colour or use. Mapping is a bit like this. The first stage is to put down all the things you think might be worth saying – not in any kind of order but just as you think of them. Then try and work out how they relate to one another and put them into some kind of logical sequence, drawing lines between the various boxes and bubbles.

You should try to do this on a blank piece of unruled paper in landscape orientation – if you do it on a ruled sheet of paper in portrait orientation, the temptation will be to write the things you think of as a list, one below the other. When you come to organize them, you will be tempted to see the order as important, rather than the order on the page simply reflecting the order in which you thought of the ideas! No, work in landscape on unruled paper and space the ideas about the page in bubbles and boxes. Then connect them into some kind of logical pattern and then, on another piece of paper, begin to work out the order of what you might say, always keeping in mind your overall aim and the people to whom you will be preaching.

Here is a suggestion about how you might set to work on your first (or next!) sermon.

## Making a start

There are few things as intimidating as a blank piece of paper. Here's a suggestion:

- Read several times the Bible passage from which you are going to preach;
- take a sheet of unruled paper and turn it sideways into 'landscape' mode;
- draw a box in the middle of the page and write in it what will be the main theme of the sermon;
- let your imagination play with the theme and draw bubbles on the page with these ideas noted in them – reflections, stories, metaphors, questions, and so on;
- as I've already said, don't try and organize where these bubbles appear on the page unless the connection to another bubble is obvious – just write down your ideas;
- check that you are still satisfied with the main idea and then think about how you are going to communicate it persuasively;
- at this point you might like to look at one or two Bible commentaries just to make sure that the way you are using the biblical material is fair and reasonable;
- begin to draw lines between the bubbles and from these connections start outlining on another piece of paper the thought progression of your sermon (you might prefer to use a pair of scissors and cut up the paper into the various ideas and physically arrange – and rearrange – them on a table);
- start placing the stories and units of thought in the order you think you will preach them;
- pay particular attention to how you will catch the congregation's attention in the opening and what message you want to leave with them at the close;

- now write the first draft of a full script;
- read the script aloud and edit those phrases which are too literary and don't sound natural when spoken to the people you envisage being in the congregation, especially avoiding jargon or long words;
- decide whether you are going to use the full script or notes, and prepare what you will have in front of you for preaching, making sure it is large enough for you to read easily when you glance down;
- read the script, or practise from the notes again before preaching;
- afterwards, welcome constructive feedback and ask people you respect for their comments, so that you can learn with practice and develop as a confident and engaging preacher.

---

### Exercise

Try and do this now! Work with a biblical passage (either one that you will be using in the future or one of the six from the exercises in the previous chapter) and go through the list to the point just before writing a full script.

When you have done it, think about what was helpful and what point you found hardest.

---

## From there to here

These are general guidelines to get you started, but there is more than one challenge in preaching. We have looked briefly at distinguishing between the content and the method, and this is good general advice. However, there is a more specific method which links the 'what' and the 'how' which some people find very helpful, and which may work for you, at least sometimes.

The method is proposed by the Canadian writer, Paul Scott Wilson, and is called 'The Four Pages of the Sermon' (see Figure 2). It doesn't give you detailed instructions as to what illustrations or quotes you should use, but it does two things very well. First, it helps you discern what might be

**The Four Pages of the Sermon**

- Bad news in the text
- Bad news in the world
- Good news in the text
- Good news in the world

**Figure 2**

God's word to the congregation in your reading of God's word and, second, it helps you organize what you might say based on this.

Hermeneutics is the art of interpretation and, while you don't need to know what various experts have said about the theory of interpretation, you do need to interpret Scripture in a way which makes sense and builds up your listeners. Yes, Christians believe the Bible is the word of God, but we still need to ask each time we read it what God is saying to us on that occasion. The answer will vary, perhaps each time, but it will certainly be influenced by what we know of the congregation to which we are going to preach. What are their pastoral needs, what are the issues facing them individually and collectively? In the light of such questions, we ask, 'What is God saying to us today through this reading?' This is hermeneutics!

Paul Scott Wilson offers a creative way through these challenges. He invites us to ask four questions and, as an alternative to the method I outlined above, to put the answers to each on a different piece of paper – the four pages.

1 **What is the bad news in the text?** What human need or situation is being addressed by the Bible reading?
2 **What is the bad news in the world?** That is, our world. What are the corresponding issues today and for your congregation which relate to the issues addressed by the Bible reading?
3 **What is the good news in the text?** How does the Bible reading provide hope for the human needs or circumstances which you have identified as 'bad news'? What is gospel here? What is the good news of how God responds to these problems and needs?
5 **What is the good news in the world?** In the light of the good news proclaimed in the text, what is that good news for today? What are God's promises, or how does our understanding of God in this text encourage us to see hope and new beginnings in our situation?

Now this is a formula which will work sometimes, but cannot be used in every circumstance, nor for every Bible reading. Nonetheless it is flexible – you can shuffle the pages, as Figure 3 illustrates. You might want to start with a problem facing the congregation and then turn to the corresponding situation in the reading, or you might want to start by celebrating the good news of the text before working through. Normally, though, you will end with good news in the world.

In addition, this method encourages us to focus on positive good news without ignoring the problems and issues which face us all in living the Christian life.

Let's look at an example of how all this might work. Let's look at a Bible reading, say Acts chapter 10, the story of Peter and Cornelius. Peter has a vision in which he is told not to restrict what he eats, but to accept all food as created by God, and therefore good. He is invited to Cornelius' house – the home of a gentile and therefore ritually unclean – and he realizes that the vision has been preparing him for this moment, an embracing of a gentile seeker after God

### Shuffling the Four Pages

- Bad news in the world
- Bad news in the text
- Good news in the text
- Good news in the world

OR:

- Good news in the text
- Bad news in the text
- Bad news in the world
- Good news in the world

**Figure 3**

and that 'God has no favourites' (verse 34). The four pages might look something like this:

- **Bad news in the world:** we live in a divided world in which conflict and suspicion keep people apart.
- **Bad news in the text:** the Jews saw gentiles as threats rather than fellow children of God, people to be excluded rather than welcomed.
- **Good news in the text:** Peter discovered that God is the God of all creation and that the good news of Jesus Christ is for all people, not only those he considered to be the 'insiders'.
- **Good news in the world:** the gospel is for all people, irrespective of race or religious practice. God's love reaches everywhere and everyone.

Of course, you could start with the Bible story, bad news in the text, or even good news in the text, but people are likely to be more attentive if you begin where they are and lead them to God and God's hope for their situation – through the pages of Scripture and your sermon.

---

### Exercise

Take the same biblical passage you worked on earlier in this chapter. This time use the 'Four Page' method to sketch out a sermon.

How does the result compare with the earlier sketched-out sermon? Are there differences? Which one will you use to produce the final sermon, or will you combine both?

---

## Preaching for a Response

**Question:** What is the worst question a preacher could be asked after they have delivered their sermon?

**Answer:** 'So what?'

It is vital that you have some idea, not only of the main theme of your sermon, but what kind of response on the part of the hearers you think would be appropriate. So, for example, in the sample four pages above on the story of Peter and Cornelius, we need to ask what we believe the appropriate response should be on the part of the congregation. We have announced that God's love reaches all people and all situations – that is good news – but what does it mean for the congregation? Perhaps it will encourage a more inclusive approach to church life, or a more open and imaginative approach to mission in the neighbourhood, or a recommitment to seeking healthy community relations between local ethnic groups. For someone in the congregation, it may speak to them of how God's love reaches out to them personally, despite what they see as their own unworthiness.

It is important that you try and imagine all these possible applications, not because you need to labour each one, but because it will help you be both suggestive and open-ended in your sermon ending. Leave the Holy Spirit to apply the message to individual hearts, but point the hearers to possible meanings for them.

This leads to an important aspect of any sermon – how it relates to the rest of the service. Once you have imagined what the possible responses might be, you can plan the prayers or songs or whatever are going to follow the sermon.

It is very important to plan ahead beyond the sermon. Ask yourself, 'What comes next?' This will help you lead the congregation in an appropriate way in the worship which immediately follows the sermon and it will also help you come to a good ending for the sermon – because you know where you are going.

## Be positive

I hope that some of these practical suggestions prove helpful as you begin to learn the art of preaching. But after these nuts and bolts, it is important to remember that preaching is about God. The most important message is not one which exhorts the congregation to try harder, but one which reminds them of the grace and love of God.

It is also important to include yourself in the message of the sermon. Never say 'you' to the congregation – always say 'we' and 'us'. Any communication which takes place in the sermon should be within a relationship of solidarity, in which you identify with the congregation. The authority is not your authority but God's, and you are as much in need of his help as is the congregation.

Remember that while the ideas will be yours, the message will be God's. People haven't gathered to hear your pearls of wisdom, but to be addressed by the life-giving, life-changing gospel of Jesus Christ. If this intimidates you, it should. All we can do is pray and offer God our weakness and readiness to listen for his voice. Then he can use us – not because we are great preachers, but because he is a gracious God.

---

### Exercise

Write your own definition of what you believe preaching to be and then compose a prayer asking for God's help as you seek to learn how to preach.

---

# 15

# Celebrating around the table

Aim: To explore something of the meaning of the Lord's Supper in order to help our leading of or participation in it.

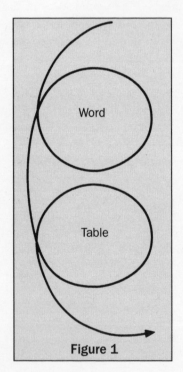

**Figure 1**

As Christians gather for worship week by week, they seek to meet God through prayer and Scripture. We have seen how the progression of that worship event can be described as a journey and can be represented by a single spiral: the congregation gathers for praise and then gathers around God's word. From this encounter with God, the worshippers are sent out as witnesses to the kingdom of God and as followers of Jesus Christ.

But there is something missing from this picture – and many would say that there is something essential missing. For a majority of Christians around the world, their weekly gathering for worship is not only a gathering around the word of God, but a gathering around the Lord's Table (see Figure 1). In much, if not most, Christian worship, the Eucharist is the central feature. It has different names in different parts of the Church: Catholics call it 'the Mass', Orthodox call it 'the Divine Liturgy', others call it 'Holy Communion', and others 'the Lord's Supper'. All agree that it is very important, though they differ in the way this is expressed. So some say that it is so important that it should be celebrated every Sunday (or even every day), while others say it is so important it should be kept for special occasions. My own free church tradition tends to celebrate it monthly for each regular service (for example, morning or evening) which a congregation holds. Although in the past, the Lord's Supper (as that is what I shall call it here) was celebrated as a short service after a main service of the word, it is now nearly always part of the main church service. So once a month there is not only a gathering around the word, but a gathering around the table.

## A means of grace

Not only do Christians differ in the frequency with which they celebrate the Eucharist (a word which means 'thanksgiving' and which is used as a generic term across the churches – alongside whichever title is used within each tradition) but they differ in their interpretation of what it means and what they believe happens in it. The word which has most commonly been used to describe what all this is about is 'sacrament', the same word which is used to refer to baptism. But still there is diversity about what that word means.

Behind the original Latin word which is usually translated 'sacrament' there lies the sense of 'an oath of allegiance', and this theme of dedication is still a part of the spirituality of the Eucharist. The main area of disagreement, however, is in what people believe God is doing in and through the eucharistic actions and the bread and wine. This isn't the place to review all the debates or disagreements, so I will focus first on my own understanding of what is happening, and then offer some basic guidance on how we might set about leading a service.

We have already seen how the worship event is not only what we do, but is a meeting with God in which God is also at work. The Holy Spirit is drawing us into worship and inspiring our prayers and touching our hearts, interpreting Scripture and transforming lives. God uses what we do to act in us and through us. The same is true of the Lord's Supper: through bread and wine, God comes close to us. Indeed, God promises to come close when we do these things – they are 'a means of grace'. This is why sometimes Baptism and the Lord's Supper are called 'ordinances', because we are obeying God when we do them – and obedience brings blessing. God is faithful and promises to meet us in his word and at his table if we come in faith and repentance.

There are three other things I want to say about sacraments. First, they are a material means by which spiritual things happen. God is the creator, and in the Lord's Supper he uses matter – bread and wine – to come close to us. This helps us to see that God is always trying to work through material means – after all, he did make the world. Our own lives are also, in some sense, sacramental, because God wants to work through our own, living flesh and blood. That's why the way we behave has spiritual significance – being disciples of Jesus day by day is a spiritual activity, but it is worked out in the rough and tumble of the material world. So the supper, and baptism, help us to see that God is not apart from the world, but intimately involved in it. So when we eat bread, we taste and chew and swallow it, and we believe that God uses that action and that experience as a way of coming close to us.

Second, it is important that when we talk about the meaning of the sacraments, that we do not only look at material elements – bread, wine and water – but that we think about what we do with them. In other words, the actions and words we use are a part of the sacrament and its meaning. For example, as a Baptist, I believe that the immersing of a new Christian in water is a part of the meaning of the sacrament of baptism, as we are buried with Christ and raised to new life in union with him.

In the Lord's Supper, the act of gathering in fellowship is a part of the symbolic meal, and the fact that this gathering is centred on Jesus Christ is a sign that the Church as a reconciled community is constituted through what God has done in Christ. In addition, the sincere offering of ourselves to God as we take bread and wine are important aspects of what is going on, and to try and explain the meaning of the supper without taking into account our sincerity could well lead to seeing the significance of the bread and wine in an almost magical way. This is why we are invited to examine our hearts before sharing in the Lord's Supper, and why our making peace with one another is also important.

Third, the sacraments point us to Jesus Christ. Baptism and the supper are not only commanded by Jesus, but are centred on Jesus. In baptism, we follow his example and we enter into union with him in his death and resurrection. In the supper, we do these things in memory of him, and his cross and resurrection are brought to the heart of our worship and are even taken into our bodies as we eat and drink. To gather around the table is to gather around Jesus Christ and to celebrate the gospel, which is only good news because of him.

## From Last Supper to Lord's Supper

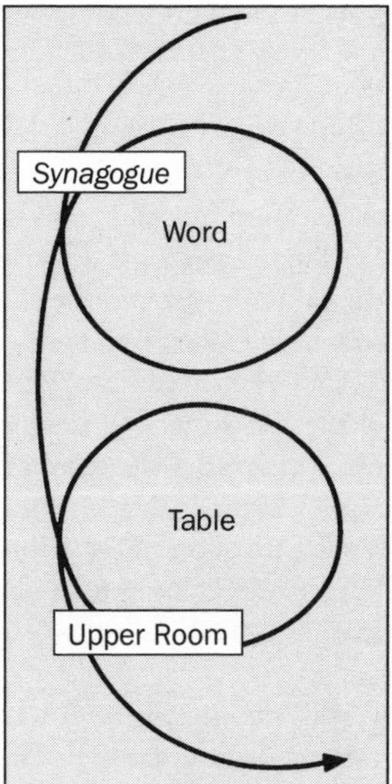

The worship of the early Christians was shaped by two particular influences. First there was the influence of the synagogue. The very first Christians were all Jews, and their worship was a natural development of what they had known when they went to the synagogue for a service made up of psalms, prayers, Scripture readings and a sermon. The worship we have explored so far in this book is directly descended from this synagogue worship, a gathering around the word

The second influence was the story of the upper room in the hours before Jesus was arrested. There he shared a Passover meal with his disciples and gave it new meaning through taking bread and wine and linking them to the meaning of his imminent death. Because he said 'Do this in memory of me', the re-enacting of that last supper has become a central feature of how Christians gather to worship God and open themselves to the influence of Jesus. On the day of Pentecost, Acts 2.42 tells us, 'They devoted themselves to the apostles' teaching and fellowship, to the breaking of bread and the prayers', a gathering around the table.

However, this was far more than simply the remembering of a past event. After the resurrection, Jesus shared a meal with the disciples on more than one occasion. In the story of his appearing to two disciples on the road to Emmaus, Luke tells us that the two hurried back to Jerusalem to tell the other disciples, 'what had happened on the road, and how he had been made known to them in the breaking of the bread' (Luke 24.35). After the resurrection, Christians soon discovered that when they obeyed Jesus and shared bread and wine in memory of him, it was far more than a memory that they experienced. Even after the ascension, they would speak of the living presence of Jesus Christ being made known 'in the breaking of bread'.

This is why the Lord's Supper was seen as much as a testimony to the resurrection of Jesus as it was a reminder of the death of Jesus, and why it soon became a central feature of weekly Sunday worship. The

Figure 2

'Last Supper' had become 'the Lord's Supper'. Christians gathered in the name of Jesus on the day of resurrection to worship God through psalms, prayers, Scripture and proclamation – and through the sharing of bread and wine, the Lord's Supper. Both the gathering around Scripture and the gathering around the table were, and are, centred on Jesus Christ. Even before the New Testament writings became 'Scripture', the Old Testament Scriptures were read in the light of Jesus and interpreted as preparation for, and explanation of, God's saving action, which reached its climax in Jesus the Christ. The gathering around the Scriptures and the gathering around the table are both activities which are aimed at encountering God, who is revealed to us in Jesus Christ.

The way in which different Christian churches have used the story of the last supper in their celebrating of the Eucharist has differed. In many cases, the words of Paul in 1 Corinthians 11 are quoted as a part of the prayer of thanksgiving. Alternatively, the free church tradition has tended to quote these 'words of institution' as an introduction to the Lord's Supper by providing a narrative framework and a setting of the scene:

> For I received from the Lord what I also handed on to you, that the Lord Jesus on the night when he was betrayed took a loaf of bread, and when he had given thanks, he broke it and said, "This is my body that is for you. Do this in remembrance of me." In the same way he took the cup also, after supper, saying, "This cup is the new covenant in my blood. Do this, as often as you drink it, in remembrance of me." For as often as you eat this bread and drink the cup, you proclaim the Lord's death until he comes.
>
> (1 Corinthians 11.23–26)

What follows is a kind of re-enactment of that last supper which Jesus shared with the disciples and in which he gave clues as to the significance of his impending death. This is all transformed in the light of the resurrection, yet our rejoicing in the risen life of Christ is still earthed in the death which made it possible.

Bread and wine therefore have double meanings. On the one hand, they are a reminder of the body which was broken, and the life blood which was shed for our salvation. On the other hand, they are signs of the living Christ, who is the bread of life and on whom we feed in faith, and the new life of the kingdom of God which we are called to celebrate and live.

## Shaping the supper

The sacraments rely on symbolism. If the bread and wine are signs which God uses to come close to us, then it is important that they have a prominent place in our worship. It is also important how they are presented to the congregation. A service may be very informal, yet the bread and the wine should still be handled, presented and shared in a reverent manner. Of course, reverence and solemnity are not the same thing, although people have often celebrated the Lord's Supper in a manner which is far from celebratory. Quiet reflection is an important part of receiving the bread and the wine, yet the drama of our salvation is also a cause for celebration. Both moods should be encouraged, just as light and shade belong together in any picture which has a strong impact on the viewer.

---

### Exercise

Back in Chapter 6 I suggested you write down all the different things that might be part of a service of worship. This time, I want you to write down, again on individual pieces of paper, all the different parts which could come in that section of the service when we celebrate the Lord's Supper – normally after the sermon.

Look through your pieces of paper – which of these do you think are essential and should be in every communion service?

---

There will be considerable variety between the way in which different congregations celebrate the Lord's Supper. Yet there are a number of core elements which need to be present. You may have identified in the exercise above various aspects which you think are essential. For me, four core elements are always necessary:

- words of institution
- prayer of thanksgiving
- breaking of bread
- sharing of bread and wine.

You may have quite a number of other things written down which may happen normally or occasionally in your church, but this is what we can call the core actions of the Lord's Supper. The words of institution (usually from 1 Corinthians 11 but sometimes from one of the Gospels) are read or recited, and this locates what we are doing as a re-enactment of the events in the upper room, when Jesus said, 'Do this in memory of me.' It is more than re-enactment, but that is where it starts, and this is where the symbolism gains its first layer of meaning.

This is followed by a prayer of thanksgiving, like grace at a meal. Jesus gave thanks for bread and wine, and we do the same – but we also go further and give thanks for Jesus himself. The prayer will often offer more than just thanksgiving, ending with a request that the Holy Spirit draw us closer to God and open our hearts to receive Christ afresh.

The breaking of the bread, at one level, is a purely functional action in which the bread is broken so that it can be shared. Yet the act of breaking also points towards the violence of Jesus' death and the Christian experience that the risen Christ becomes known 'in the breaking of bread'.

The sharing of bread and wine may happen in different ways. Stewards may distribute the elements to the congregation who remain seated in their places, as at a meal. Alternatively, the congregation may come forward to receive the elements, although this tends to happen in more liturgical denominations. Either way, this is the point at which the bread and wine, which have been a central focus of the worship of the gathered congregation, are received by each member of it. The communal experience of worship should always have an individual dimension of personal devotion, and this is particularly true in the receiving of bread and wine. Here is an opportunity for personal thanksgiving and a rededication of the worshipper as a follower of Jesus Christ. The sharing of the bread is also a sign of the unity of the congregation as they eat of the one loaf (1 Corinthians 10.17).

In addition to these core elements, here are a number of other components in a service of the Lord's Supper that I would put down on pieces of paper. You might compare them with yours.

1   There will often be words of introduction and welcome such as:

> Come to this table, not because you must but because you may,
> not because you are strong, but because you are weak.
> Come, not because any goodness of your own gives you a right to
> come, but because you need mercy and help.
> Come, because you love the Lord a little and would like to love him
> more.
> Come, because he loved you and gave himself for you.
> Come and meet the risen Christ, for we are his Body.
>
> (Ellis and Blyth, *Gathering for Worship*, p. 14)

2 Scripture sentences may be used such as:

> Jesus said to them, 'I am the bread of life.
> Whoever comes to me will never be hungry,
> and whoever believes in me will never be thirsty.'

(John 6.35)

3 Sometimes the peace will be shared as the members of the congregation are invited to greet one another. This is more than a simple greeting, as the context of the Lord's Supper reminds us that our fellowship with one another is made possible by our being forgiven by God through the cross and by our forgiving of one another.

4 After the sharing of the bread and wine, there will often be words of acclamation such as the traditional phrase:

> Christ has died,
> Christ is risen,
> Christ will come again!

5 A further prayer asking for God's help in our living as faithful followers of Christ could follow.

A simple pattern for the Lord's Supper may look like this:

Scripture sentences
Invitation
Sharing the Peace (or some other sign of fellowship)
**Word of institution**
**Prayer of thanksgiving**
**Breaking of bread**
**Sharing of bread and wine**
Acclamation
Prayer

There may be variations on this, though the core elements should be there. In the book *Gathering for Worship*, there are a number of patterns offered as resources for worship leaders and congregations. There is what is called a 'simple pattern', which is very similar to what is printed here, but there is also a pattern which uses storytelling, one which uses prayers and other words from the world church, one which focuses on reconciliation and a pattern which expresses the concern for kingdom living,

> ### Exercise
>
> Picking up the idea of impro-
> vising, play with the different
> pieces of paper, creating differ-
> ent patterns and shapes. Note
> down the shapes you form and
> also how you think this might
> influence and effect the way the
> congregation experiences the
> Lord's Supper.
>
> For example, what might be the
> difference in placing the peace
> after bread and wine are shared,
> rather than beforehand?

with an emphasis on justice and peace. Yet each begins with the upper room and, in the presence of the risen Christ, gives thanks, breaks bread and shares bread and wine. Indeed, the possibilities for exploring different ways of celebrating the Lord's Supper are increased once we ensure that the core elements are present – rather like a jazz group improvising freely because they all know the basic tune or chord progression, which gives them the freedom to extemporize.

## The Supper of the Lord

The Lord's Supper is a sacrament and as such is full of symbolism. We cannot fully explain what the symbolism stands for – or else, we might just as well use words in the first place. Just as we might hold a jewel up to the light and, as we turn it, different facets reveal different aspects of its beauty, so on various occasions, various aspects of the Lord's Supper will come to the fore. In a time of conflict, the theme of peace will be important, in a hurting community the theme of forgiveness will be strik-ing, and at other times our own response will be marked by rededication, thanksgiving for God's love or simply comfort in the faithful presence of God.

On certain occasions, the leader can guide some of this. On Christmas Eve, the mystery of the incarnation is highlighted, not only by the mid-night hour, but by God's presence mediated to us by bread and wine, which point to the newly born flesh and blood of the babe in Bethlehem. On Easter Day, the church can celebrate that the Christ who was cruci-fied and buried is now alive and present for us as we eat bread and drink wine.

In closing this chapter, let's look at some of the main themes that will be expressed in the Lord's Supper, even though the one most prominent for us may differ from occasion to occasion. Yet, even as we explore the diverse meanings of the supper, we must begin with what all these mean-ings have in common – or rather, who these meanings have in common

– because all the meanings refer back to Jesus Christ, who is at the heart of the supper. It is the supper of the Lord, and all the symbolism finds its meaning in him.

'Do this in memory of me' suggests that the supper is backward-looking, a remembrance of a time past. But this is not the whole story, for in biblical terms, to remember is to make present as well as to look back. This church building becomes the upper room, this community of disciples becomes the disciples, and the presence at the table is the presence of the one who first broke bread, before his own body was broken, buried and raised.

Sometimes, the Lord's Supper is called 'a gospel sacrament' because it embodies the gospel of Jesus Christ, and this gospel can be expressed in different ways. It is a gospel of forgiveness, in which we rejoice that our sins are forgiven and, at the table, we give thanks for this release and seek God's help in our forgiving of others. It is a gospel of reconciliation, in which we are reconciled with God and with others. At the table, we express this reconciliation by sharing the peace, or by praying for the needs of the church fellowship. It is a gospel of love, in which we are transformed by God's prior love for us. At the table, we respond to that love, especially its costly sacrifice in the cross of Christ, and open ourselves to communion with our risen Lord. It is a gospel which creates communities of reconciled men and women. At the table, we give thanks that we are called to be the body of Christ, and that each one of us is enlisted in a ministry of reconciliation in a divided world. It is a gospel of hope, and, at the table, we look forward to God's kingdom, praying for justice and peace, and sometimes contributing money for the needs of the poor.

To use another musical image, here is a theme and variations. The variations are many, as the Holy Spirit ministers to our differing needs and circumstances. But the theme is constant, and should always be recognizable, for it is the supper of the Lord:

Christ has died,
Christ is risen,
Christ will come again!

# 16

# Wider horizons

> Aim: To recognize the value of learning from worship practices from beyond the free church tradition.

Although I hope that a wide range of readers will find this book helpful, it was first planned as an attempt to help those who are beginning to lead worship in what is sometimes called 'the free churches'. In other words, the worship which we have been exploring has been that which does not normally use a set prayer book and which requires detailed planning on the part of the worship leader. Sometimes this is called 'non-liturgical' worship but, although most people might know what I mean, I am uneasy about using that particular label.

So what is 'liturgical' worship? The word itself is fairly elastic and can be used in both a general and a specific way. Used as a general term, it can simply be another word for 'worship' – so I could call myself 'a worship specialist' or, alternatively, 'a liturgical specialist'. Similarly, this general sense lies behind the term 'liturgical theology', a discipline which uses the words and actions of worship in order to explore what the church believes. However, the specific, or narrower, use of 'liturgical' refers to a particular type of worship: the sort that is found in the Anglican, Roman Catholic, Lutheran and Eastern Orthodox churches. This kind of worship has a number of common characteristics, although not all of them will apply to each church I have just mentioned. Mark Earey in his *Liturgical Worship*, has produced a list which includes:

- The use of service books – usually approved by a central denominational authority – though some modern congregations might use big screens or leaflets in providing the words for the congregation.
- Words for the congregation to join in saying or singing, apart from hymns and songs.
- A building or worship space with clearly symbolic furniture.
- The use of symbolic actions and objects, such as processions, lighted candles or incense.
- The use of special clothes by those leading worship.
- The giving of names to particular Sundays, marking points in the Christian year.

Free church worship has, in its historical development, often taken forms which have been self-conscious attempts to be as different from this liturgical worship as possible. In particular, it has been suspicious of symbols and visual ways of focusing the attention of the congregation, such as with a cross or crucifix. It has also been suspicious of prayer books, believing that prayer should be spontaneous and free. However, the ecumenical movement has led to far closer fellowship and co-operation between different Christian traditions, and this has resulted not only in much shared worship, but in an increasing willingness to learn from one another. For the free churches, this has meant a readiness to use in their worship some of the resources and methods which come from other parts of the Christian Church. We will explore the Christian year in the next chapter but, for now, we shall look briefly at some of the possible uses of other liturgical material and ways of worshipping.

## Congregational readings and responses

The congregation saying or singing things, apart from hymns and songs, is a central feature of liturgical worship, whether from a prayer book, some other written source, or from memorized material. While this has sometimes been seen as too 'formal' by some free church people, it actually gives the congregation a larger part to play in worship and enables greater participation on the part of all the worshippers.

The most common example of this is the congregation saying together the words of a prayer, a psalm or a creed. This might either be a block of material which it says together or it may be arranged antiphonally, that is, in a responsive manner. Either the leader says something to which the congregation responds, or the material may be arranged for different sections of the congregation to say different parts. Either way, this encourages a sense of participation and dialogue which many would see as a richer experience of worship than the congregation simply listening to someone at the front saying the words on its behalf.

These words may be from the Bible, whether a psalm or some other passage such as the Magnificat (Luke 1.46–55), the Benedictus (Luke 1.68–79) or the song of the servant king (Philippians 2.5–11). Indeed, many passages may be arranged for congregational use and the use of data projectors, overhead projectors and photocopied leaflets makes the practicalities fairly straightforward, as we saw in Chapter 12.

Don't assume that the material is simply arranged in alternate verses but read it through and decide which voices might say each section. Here is an example from the end of Psalm 118. You will notice that I haven't followed the verse divisions, but have tried to arrange according to what will make sense as a responsive reading:

This is the gate of the Lord;
   **the righteous shall enter through it.**

I thank you that you have answered me
   and have become my salvation.

**The stone that the builders rejected**
   **has become the chief cornerstone.**

This is the Lord's doing;
   it is marvellous in our eyes.

**This is the day that the Lord has made;**
   **let us rejoice and be glad in it.**

Save us, we beseech you, O Lord!
   **O Lord, we beseech you, give us success!**

**Blessed is the one who comes in the name of the Lord.**
   **We bless you from the house of the Lord.**

The Lord is God,
   and he has given us light.
Bind the festal procession with branches,
   up to the horns of the altar.

**You are my God, and I will give thanks to you;**
   **you are my God, I will extol you.**

**O give thanks to the Lord, for he is good,**
   **for his steadfast love endures forever.**

Alternatively, you might tweak the words of Scripture and turn them into a prayer. Here is an example using a selection of verses from Romans 12.1–17, a passage which is not arranged antiphonally, but for the whole congregation to say as a prayer of consecration:

Holy God,
I present my body to you as a living sacrifice,
holy and acceptable, my spiritual worship.
Strengthen me today,
that I might not be conformed to this world,
but transformed by the renewing of my mind,
that I may discern your will –
what is good and acceptable and perfect.

Help me Lord,
make my love genuine;
hating evil and holding fast to what is good.
By your Spirit, open my heart to the risen Lord Jesus,
that I might bless those who persecute me,
rejoice with those who rejoice
and mourn with those who mourn.
Do not let me repay anyone evil for evil,
but make me an instrument of the peace of Christ,
in whose name I pray.

Obviously you must be sensitive when altering words from the Bible! But in this example Paul wrote the original as an exhortation to his readers. All I have done here is turn that exhortation into a prayer of commitment – the natural response to Paul's words.

Simpler examples would be the use of traditional prayer responses such as:

Lord, in your mercy:
Hear our prayer

or:

Lord, have mercy
Christ, have mercy
Lord, have mercy

or, at Easter:

The Lord is risen!
He is risen indeed. Halleluiah!

It is good sometimes to write new words for the congregation to use as a response to a prayer, but always remember the importance of the original congregational response – **Amen!**

Space does not allow further examples but, before we move on, let's note clearly what such congregational words achieve. First, they give the congregation an additional opportunity to contribute actively to the worship. Second, they enable the members of the congregation to say these words together. Third, they enable a more interactive style of prayer or proclamation, in which a dialogue between leader and congregation, or between sections of the congregation, can bring to life words of Scripture.

## Drama, movement and sacred space

Many churches are discovering the power of drama in their worship, whether it is a dramatized Bible reading with different voices, or the use of sketches to communicate important ideas or provide proactive means of communication. But there are other ways in which drama can provide a dimension to worship. For example, the way a sermon is preached might be very dramatic if the preacher is enthusiastic and gifted. It might even take the form of storytelling or a dialogue.

But there can also be drama built into the way the service is led – through the use of contrast (such as celebration followed by silence) or the use of movement. This movement may be the ministry of a dance group, or the contribution of a flag-waver. Or it may be a procession of singers and congregation, for example, children and others processing around the church building on Palm Sunday while singing songs such as Graham Kendrick's 'Make way'. In liturgical traditions, the use of ritual movement has often been important – whether it is kneeling for prayer, making of the sign of the cross, or moving to different parts of the church during worship. So, for example, in some churches, when the Gospel is read, the Bible is carried into the middle of the congregation and all the worshippers stand and turn inwards towards the Bible. This is a powerful symbol of being attentive to God's word, and of the whole church being shaped by the good news of Jesus Christ.

Some church buildings are very plain in appearance and functional in design, simply offering an auditorium in which a congregation can meet and leaders can be heard. But many buildings in the more liturgical churches are designed as sacred space, in which even the layout of the building suggests our reverent approach to the holy God. Altar steps and communion rails, soaring ceilings and stained glass can all help to give the worshippers a sense that this is a special place where they gather to encounter Almighty God.

Of course, others prefer a simpler, less formal approach to church architecture. The point is not which is right, but how can we use the space available to help people to worship?

---

### Exercise

Make a sketch of the worship area of your church or the building you use on a Sunday. What does its layout and style say about what that church thinks is important?

Now imagine you can move the chairs (even if they happen to be pews!) and even other features of the building. What configuration would you prefer normally and why? What symbolism does this suggest? What other arrangements might be more appropriate for other specific occasions?

---

## Visual symbols

We live in an increasingly visual culture. More and more we recognize the power of symbols to communicate truth, persuade us to think in particular ways and motivate us to action. Whether it's the image of a sporting icon, the familiarity of a marketing logo or the power of television and cinema, we know that what we see stimulates our imagination and stirs our desires. Again, the free church tradition has known this and, historically, has been suspicious of it. A fear of idolatry has meant that this tradition has sought simple worship but, as a result, has tended to produce abstract worship full of words and ideas.

However, this is one area where the ecumenical movement has had a particularly powerful effect, as contact with other Christians has led to an appreciation of their worship, and a recognition that God can speak to us through what we see, as well as what we read or hear. Evangelicals have even begun to appreciate Orthodox icons, as the ancient tradition of meditating upon God through the representation of biblical characters and stories has been explored. Contact with fellow Christians has led many to discover how helpful a cross can be as a focus of prayer or worship and how evocative and spiritually moving can be the use of colour and the powerful symbolism of artistic creativity.

So how might an awareness of visual communication help the leading of worship? First, we must realize that people are different in temperament and emotion. Some will be very keen to receive in worship expositions of Scripture and lucid explanations of Christian doctrine. They may be indifferent to music, or indeed to what they see. Others will be moved by music, and yet others will be helped by having a visual focus to gain and keep their attention. These latter worshippers may be distracted by clutter at the front of the church, but stimulated by simple images or the use of evocative lighting. A simple candle flame may be enough to help them give attention to God and be open to the still voice within. The use of photographs, video clips or digital animations may each touch some worshippers in a more powerful way than the preacher.

The worship leader needs to try and reach each of the different personality types which make up a congregation, and so the wider range of resources that are available the better. Enriching worship through the visual is an important opportunity to honour our creator God through artistic creativity, and to serve a section of our congregations by communicating to them at a deeper level than we would be able to do merely by using words.

## Multi-sensory worship

In exploring the use of visual media we have already been thinking about multi-sensory worship. We have five senses, yet traditionally we have only used speech and hearing. But the use of our eyes, of touch and smell, can all help us to worship more creatively and wholeheartedly. To light a candle in a darkened church while singing a simple song or chant can help many to sense God's presence. Now if that candle is scented, it would draw in a further sense, or if there are many candles and the worshippers are invited to hold them or carry them and place them before the cross, then we can movingly present Jesus as the light of the world – the light that has shone and which the darkness has not overcome.

If we invite people to write down on a piece of paper their regrets and the things of which they wish to repent, and then if those pieces of paper are burned and God's forgiveness declared, then this may reach people who are unmoved by a sermon on forgiveness.

Each Christmas, the church which I pastor has a Christmas tree in the sanctuary. No great symbolism in that and certainly it is not as evocative as the Advent candles which are lit week by week. But after Christmas the tree is stripped and during Lent it appears in the church fashioned into the shape of a large cross. Christmas and Easter are linked. The incarnation, God with us, results in God being with us in death as well as life. The babe of Bethlehem becomes the man who is acquainted with grief, and by whose stripes we are healed. For Easter Sunday the cross is covered with mesh, the worshippers are given a daffodil on their arrival for worship and, during the service, the whole congregation comes forward and each places their flower prayerfully on the cross. The barren wood becomes aflame with colour and a symbol of life. This practice is in no way original to our congregation and is followed in a growing number of churches but, each year, I am struck by the reflective prayerfulness and attentive devotion of those queuing to place their flower on the cross. This is multi-sensory worship.

Some of the congregation find it difficult to stand still when we are singing praise. The small children fidget, but some of the children and some of the adults move with the rhythm of the music. They clap their hands (touch and sound), they move their bodies as though breaking out in dance, and some even do dance or wave flags as an exultant offering of their whole selves, including their bodies, to God: this is multi-sensory worship.

An evening service on God's guidance and faithfulness sees the worshippers bringing stones forward and constructing a cairn as a sign of God's goodness to pilgrims and wanderers. Those who are sick come forward for the laying on of hands and prayer, as the touch of another assures them of God's grace and welcome. This is multi-sensory worship. Banners around the sanctuary, actions to the songs, embraces during the peace: this is multi-sensory worship. The distributing of palm crosses, the washing of feet and the sharing of bread and wine: this is multi-sensory worship.

The use of ideas and practices from other parts of the church is an important resource for worship leader and worshipper alike. But it is important that ideas new to a congregation are introduced sensitively, not in order to impress or amaze, but in order to help them come close to God. The guidelines in this book should help you develop principles of good worship which will enable you to draw widely on ideas new to you and

> **Exercise**
>
> Plan the outline of a service that uses senses in different ways:
>
> • using photographs
> • using light and darkness
> • using movement and touch.

your congregation, but without falling into the trap of self-indulgent gimmickry. Our God is our creator and, by definition creative. He calls us to be creative in our worship and our leading of worship.

# 17

# Time and eternity: the Christian year

> Aim: To understand how the Christian year
> provides a rich resource for Christian worship.

Sometimes people comment that a particular preacher has only one
sermon. They may change the text and even the illustrations – but they
preach the same sermon time after time. Does the same thing happen to
Sundays? The date may change, the seasons roll on, but worship is the
same week after week. One Sunday is much like another. Or is it?

From the early centuries of the Christian Church, worship has been
shaped by a sense of time, as though in time worship can represent that
which is eternally true about God. This is because Christians believe that
the eternal God has revealed himself in history – and so within time.
Through the history of Israel, from the calling of Abraham, the freeing of
the Hebrew slaves and the ups and downs of the Jewish nation, God has
been revealed as a faithful saviour and righteous judge. Supremely, in the
birth, life, death and resurrection of Jesus of Nazareth, God has acted in
history for our salvation and the redemption of all things.

We live in time and cannot escape it, however much we might try. Our
lives are made up of blocks of time: usually, we will work, rest and sleep
each day, we will try to rest for at least a day each week and, in most
parts of the world, the turning seasons are marked by lengthening and
shortening days, by warmth and cold. There is a rhythm to these variations, and from before the time of Christ these rhythms have shaped the
patterns of worship and prayer for Jews and then Christians.

The coming of light and the coming of darkness have affected the time and mood of morning and evening prayers. In most Christian traditions this has primarily been a time for personal prayer, but when Christians have lived in some kind of residential community, their common life has often been shaped around their gathering for worship at the beginning and end of each day.

From the time of the Old Testament, the Sabbath or seventh day of the week, has been for Jews a day for remembering God's completion of creation (Genesis 2.3) and has also been a day available for worship. However, by the end of the first century CE, Christians were calling the first day of the week 'the Lord's Day', for this was the day on which Jesus was raised from the dead and it became the day of weekly worship – though it was not until much later that the Roman state recognized it and it became a day when people could rest from work.

As we have looked at the connections between worship and the rest of life, we have seen how this weekly gathering for worship enables Christians to 'regroup' after the compromises and failures of the week. We need to focus on God and to pay the gospel sustained attention after a week when our attention has wandered and we have, perhaps, been beguiled by many things. Amidst the competing claims of the world, we are in danger of losing our distinctive Christian voice, and we need to sing the Lord's song again so we can regain that song in our lives. This is the rhythm of worship > engagement > worship. Remember that all rhythm, whether in music or living, is about time – and worship is about the offering of time to God and about our seeing time in a new way because of God's recreating love. Perhaps even more important than this is the truth that we offer the first day of the week to God as a sign that the whole week is truly his. Either way, this worship happens on the day of resurrection, for through that resurrection everything is different, in heaven and on earth, in time and in eternity.

In addition to these daily and weekly rhythms, there are the changing seasons. For most of the history of the church, Christians have followed a sequence of special days which have been associated with parts of the drama of salvation. Many evangelical Christians don't follow this sequence of special days in much detail, perhaps just Christmas and Easter. But in recent years more and more attention has been paid to the Christian year, as people have discovered in it a rich resource for worship and personal devotion, both in its themes and in its power to draw worshippers into the story of our salvation.

## Telling the story

The story of our salvation is the story of Jesus, and so it is quite natural that congregations which gather week by week 'in the name of Jesus' should configure the themes of that worship around his story. From a practical point of view, this cycle of special days lasts for only just over half of the year. There are plenty of weeks through the summer and autumn to follow special sermon series or do other things, but from December to June let's shape our worship with the story of Jesus.

Here is an outline of the main festivals and special days. Sometimes the dates are fixed, like Christmas Day. Sometimes they vary because the date of Sundays will change from year to year. The date of Easter is calculated according to when Passover is – and that is based on the cycles of the moon – so that date can vary between late March and late April. These festivals are a combination of seasons – periods of time – and special days, usually the focus of those seasons. So, for example, we celebrate Easter on Easter Day but we can also continue to celebrate it for the Sundays which follow – right up until Ascension and Pentecost. This gives us opportunity to go deeper in our understanding of these events, and to enter into the spirit of the story.

**Advent** marks the beginning of the Christian year. Traditionally it has been a time of fasting and personal preparation for the celebration of Christmas. It begins with Advent Sunday, which is the fourth Sunday before Christmas, when the theme is usually the second advent of Christ. Preparation of ourselves through reflection and confession begins with acknowledging that God has come in Christ – who will also return in judgement. This traditional theme may or may not be helpful on this Sunday, but many will simply mark Advent as a time of anticipation – a countdown to Christmas – in which Advent candles are lit each week and the Bible stories about John the Baptist and Mary feature prominently.

**Christmas** is, of course, 25 December and marks the birth of Jesus. We don't know the actual date, and even calculating the year is not straight-forward, but it's a kind of official birthday, a bit like Trooping the Colour is the official birthday of the British Queen. At Christmas we celebrate the beginning of the life of Jesus. But we do more than that, because we also celebrate the word made flesh, the incarnation of the eternal Son of God in human form. We rejoice in a birth, but we rejoice even more that this birth is the coming of Immanuel, God-with-us in our human exist-ence, in life and death. Increasingly, churches which are not traditionally liturgical will hold a midnight communion service on Christmas Eve, and many will gather on Christmas morning, usually for a family service to celebrate Christmas Day.

**Epiphany** is 6 January and is the twelfth day after Christmas Day, although, in the Eastern Church it is when Christmas is celebrated. Usually, this festival is associated with the coming of the wise men to Jesus. As such, it is a reminder that Jesus is the saviour of the whole world and this can lead to a focus on world mission. In some churches, Epiphany is also associated with the baptism of Jesus, and can then act as the beginning of a series of services which follow the ministry of Jesus up to Holy Week and Easter.

**Ash Wednesday** marks the beginning of **Lent**, which is a time for personal reflection and preparation for Easter. Lent has traditionally been a time of fasting, and the Scripture themes focus on the developing story of Jesus approaching Jerusalem. It contains a number of special Sundays, the first of which has nothing at all to do with Lent: Mothering Sunday is a secular festival which many churches mark as a way of celebrating the family, though sensitivity is needed because of the diverse circumstances of the people present. Passion Sunday is a day to mark the suffering of Jesus and to give thanks for God's sacrificial and costly love. It is followed by Palm Sunday which remembers the entry of Jesus into Jerusalem, and marks the beginning of Holy Week.

**Holy Week** is a time when many churches hold special weekday services, sometimes with neighbouring churches. The mood is usually reflective and the services remember the stories of Jesus leading up to the cross. The evening of Maundy Thursday is often a time when churches will celebrate the Lord's Supper, usually in a way which dramatically evokes the Last Supper in the upper room. Good Friday, of course, is the day on which Christians very specifically remember the death of Jesus, and is often marked by reflective services and vigils.

In the ancient world, a day was regarded as beginning at dusk of the previous day, rather than midnight or dawn. Consequently, **Easter Day** traditionally began at sundown on Saturday, which became a time for the Easter vigil, a service of readings and prayer that ended with communion. Some churches have revived this Saturday night vigil, but others have tended to mark sunrise on Sunday as the beginning of Easter, and some churches have gathered in the open air for a sunrise communion service. This is the day of resurrection, and the theme is celebratory and triumphant as the news of God defeating death, and the gospel of new life in Christ, is proclaimed. This theme of new life may well continue through the Sundays of the Easter season, when the various resurrection appearance stories can form the Scripture readings. Easter is such an important time that it used to be called 'the queen of festivals', and celebrating the whole season, not just Easter Day is to be recommended. All of Christianity hangs on this core truth – that Christ was dead but now he is alive and promises new life to all who put their trust in him.

**Ascension Day**, forty days after Easter Day, marks the end of Christ's life on earth and his exaltation in glory. Many free churches will not mark this festival on the Thursday, but may do so on the following Sunday, which is often known as Ascension Sunday.

**Pentecost**, or Whit Sunday, is the following week and celebrates the coming of the Holy Spirit to the early Church, recorded in the second chapter of Acts. This is a time to focus on the work of the Spirit in our lives, to be open to God's work in us and through us and to mark the birthday of the Christian Church.

**Trinity Sunday** is the following week, and this provides the climax to the cycle of special Sundays. Here the focus is on the richness of God, Father, Son and Holy Spirit, and offers an opportunity for wonder and praise, as well as trust and thankfulness. Although the story we have followed is the story of Jesus, through it God is revealed in grace and love. In the doctrine of the Trinity we see that love is not only something to be demonstrated in time, but is something which is eternally true of God.

After Trinity Sunday (and in some churches each Sunday is known as 'so many Sundays after Trinity'), there is a long period of what is called 'ordinary time'. Some churches will mark saints' days, as they will have done throughout the year, but the main festivals will have gone until we begin the cycle again in Advent. During this period, some churches will celebrate a harvest festival, perhaps a church anniversary and, in the United Kingdom, Remembrance Sunday, when the victims of war are remembered.

Recently, however, some churches have introduced what is known as 'the **Kingdom Season'**, which begins with All Saints' Day on 1 November and continues until the beginning of Advent. The last Sunday before Advent Sunday has been called 'the feast of Christ the King', and provides a good opportunity to celebrate that Jesus is Lord, before preparing to celebrate his story again.

Some denominations produce a list of Bible readings for each Sunday in the year. In more liturgical churches, these lectionaries are given considerable authority and will be followed by most, if not all, congregations. In other churches, worship leaders may well choose their own readings to relate to the themes of the Christian year, or they may use a lectionary for certain main festivals.

---

**Exercise**

Choose a Gospel and write down the dates of all the Sundays from
Epiphany to Easter next year. Now select a reading for each week
which will enable the worship to follow the ministry of Jesus through
to the cross and the resurrection. Try to ensure that each week has
a clear theme and that there is a balance of themes over the period.

---

## Entering the story

It may be that this will leave some people cold. They will observe the
main days of Christmas and Easter, but not much else. However, many
will see in these themes the opportunity to stay with the story in more
depth than is likely to happen when there is no shape or plan to the
weekly themes. This will be particularly true for people who wish to use
their imagination in worship and prayer, and who welcome the opportunity to identify with the biblical characters and events.

This is a dramatic approach to proclamation, where we invite people to
enter imaginatively into the story rather than simply hear it. Even though
we know the end of the story, there is a tension which can enter our
consciousness as we re-live the biblical events, as we anticipate special
days and as we wonder at God's love entering the fabric of our world.
Good story-telling has the capacity to draw people into the story and
the Christian year can be seen as a huge exercise in storytelling. When I
am engrossed in a story, I lose track of the time and want to know what
will happen next. With stories I have read before, I become familiar with
the characters and wonder what part I might have played if I were a
part of the drama. So my involvement with the biblical stories and my
engagement with the theological truths they communicate is enhanced
by my becoming a part of the rhythm of the Christian year – weeping
at the cross and rejoicing at the empty tomb, wondering at the mystery
of the incarnation and opening myself to the work of the Holy Sprit at
Pentecost.

This means that worship leaders should plan seasonal worship in such
a way that more than ever the worshippers are involved: children lighting
advent candles, Christmas communion crossing the threshold of mid-
night, and Easter sunrise celebrations. There are many resources available, both in books of worship material and on the internet.

## Sharing the story

So what are the advantages of following the Christian year? First, to follow the themes of the Christian year is to focus our attention on Jesus Christ in a sustained way. We don't dart in and out of our pet topics, but stay with Jesus from birth, through ministry, to cross, empty tomb and ascension. The Christian year is Christ-centred.

Second, any preacher who follows the Christian year in the choice of readings and preaching themes is likely to be more comprehensive in the doctrines they expound, and the facets of the gospel they proclaim. Pastors are called to share 'the full counsels of God', and this is a good way of touching all the bases.

Third, the year offers us a deep rhythm, a heartbeat which pulsates with the love of God through the life and death and resurrection of Jesus Christ. Here are themes of life and death, here is betrayal and faithfulness, plodding obedience and life in the Spirit, human longing and prayerful anticipation. Here is the potential for a deep engagement with Jesus – a discipleship which is marked by Scripture and prayer.

How does the preacher choose the Scripture for preaching? Some will use the language of 'being led' or something being 'laid on my heart' – but often the reality is personal preference or a series which exhorts and exhausts.

Far better is the discipline of a given text with which to struggle. If you do not want to follow a series of lectionary readings throughout the whole year – and I don't – then at least follow through from Advent to Christmas, Lent, Easter, Ascension and Pentecost. Don't parachute in on isolated stories of Jesus, but follow the story week by week, identifying with the struggles of the disciples and the saving promises of God.

You may find that as you travel in time with Jesus, the word made flesh in Bethlehem becomes flesh again in your own desires and actions – what a journey!

### Exercise

Work out what the sermon subjects/Bible readings have been in your local church for the last year (you might need to talk to someone about it). What subjects/readings have been dominant and what might have been missed out? What kind of pattern and shape has been used, and why might this have been chosen?

# Reflecting

# 18

# Dimensions of worship

Worship is about meeting God. Of course, it is more than that, because when we meet God certain things follow – we praise God, confess our sins, ask for God's help, and so on. But when we gather with other Christians for worship, the kind of event we envisage is not simply one in which we talk and sing to one another, but in which together we seek to meet God. We don't plan to talk among ourselves with God as an interested and benign eavesdropper. We go in search of God, believing that when we pray, God will hear us, that when we explore Scripture, God will address us and that when we open ourselves to God's Spirit, God will guide and transform us.

This book is called *Approaching God* for this very reason: in worship we approach the God who approaches us. In worship, we approach God with the hope of meeting the one who is the source of all life and also our own creator and saviour. But we also come knowing that the God whom we seek is the God who in grace seeks and comes close to us. In Jesus Christ he has shared our human existence and, by his Spirit, God seeks to transform, guide and work through each one of us. Even our gathering for worship is the work of God: the Holy Spirit encourages us, increasing our resolve to meet for worship and drawing us together into a worshipping community.

## Worship is for God

In this chapter we are going to explore some of the ways in which worship affects the worshippers. There are a number of positive ways in which those who gather to meet God are blessed by the encounter, and it is human nature that some of the time some of us will see this blessing as the main reason for worshipping. However, even before we examine these blessings, it's important to publish a health warning: true worship is for God.

Yes, we will benefit from worshipping – but that's the point – from worshipping! In other words, the positive benefits, or 'added value', which the worshippers gain as a result of worshipping, come from the dynamics of truly worshipping God – not simply attending a church service. Worship is for God, who is deserving of our full attention, our sacrifice of praise and our complete devotion and trust. If we set out to worship in order to gain various benefits, then we are putting ourselves at the centre of our concern, rather than God, and so are not truly worshipping God. I call this 'instrumental abuse' – which has absolutely nothing to do with the misuse of guitars, but everything to do with treating worship as a means to an end. To regard worship as an instrument is to see it as primarily the means by which we achieve various benefits for the congregation. This is self-defeating, because those benefits do not accrue unless we are truly worshipping God.

So should we see these blessings as a by-product of worship? Well, perhaps. But I believe they are more central than that. God sets things up in such a way that when we enter into our true relationship with him, that is worship. Then these other things benefit us and help us to grow and serve as Christians. This is God's economy – the way things work in the kingdom – put God first, and his kingdom and all the rest will be added to you (Matthew 6.33).

So let's explore some of these blessings which God, in his goodness, offers us through our worship – dimensions of our worship of God.

## Worship as devotion

At the heart of worship, then, is an encounter with God. This meeting is shaped by who God is, and who we are, by what God has done, and what we have done and failed to do. So we praise and confess, ask and listen. We utter prayers and sing songs, we bring gifts and we make requests. But underneath or inside these words and actions, what is going on? When we pray, either one person speaks on our behalf, as our representative, or else we read aloud the words of a shared prayer. But what is going on? Where is the prayer? Is it in the words that are read or uttered – or is it in the hearts of each member of the congregation? Well, of course, it's both. The words uttered by a worship leader can help me to pray, as can the written words of a prayer composed by someone else. But my prayer is something which I offer to God in the honesty and heartfelt devotion of my relationship with him.

This is why Scripture so often speaks about the human heart. Long before the circulatory system was understood in any scientific way, this organ of the body was seen as a symbol of the centre, or heart, of a person. To worship God with all my heart is to offer God the whole of myself, the deepest recesses of my consciousness and the deepest needs of my spirit. So Jesus announced the *Shema* of Deuteronomy 6.4–5 as the first of the commandments:

> Jesus answered, "The first is, 'Hear, O Israel: the Lord our God, the Lord is one; you shall love the Lord your God with all your heart, and with all your soul, and with all your mind, and with all your strength.' The second is this, 'You shall love your neighbour as yourself.'"
>
> (Mark 12.29–31)

While gathered worship is a communal event in which the congregation speaks and acts collectively, it is also a personal event in which each worshipper is called to seek God with the whole of their being. This 'heart worship' is a vital dimension of any true worship, and the leader should be constantly aware of the need to help people worship in a 'whole-hearted' way.

We may call this the 'devotional dimension' of worship for it is the place where each person 'does business' with God. In the secrecy of our own hearts we confess our sins and we find our spirits kindled by the grace and love of God. Here God's love seeks out our answering love, and here God's forgiveness seeks true repentance. And in the intimacy of our personal relationship with God, the Holy Spirit seeks to make us whole and increase within us the capacity to love, and the desire to love God more. In the words of Charles Wesley:

> O thou who camest from above
>     the pure, celestial fire to impart,
> kindle a flame of sacred love
>     on the mean altar of my heart.
>
> There let it for thy glory burn
>     with inextinguishable blaze;
> and, trembling, to its source return
>     in humble love and fervent praise.

We have described the progression of a service as being like a journey with God. But people also use the picture of a journey to talk of their life-long experience of God and his working in their lives. In this personal pilgrimage, the encounter with God in worship will often provide significant moments, landmarks, which will be visible when the person looks back on that journey. In worship, a person may come to faith. In worship, a person may make a special commitment to God in response to a vocational challenge. In worship a person may face up to some aspect of truth about their life, and cry on God for help. It is not that these things don't happen outside worship, such as in personal prayers or moments of personal crisis. But in worship, we are paying attention to God in a special and sustained way and this inevitably leads to moments of devotional intensity which can prove significant for the whole of our lives.

Jesus told the Samaritan woman, 'God is spirit, and those who worship him must worship in spirit and truth' (John 4.24). This is devotional worship, and without such devotion we don't have true worship – however wonderful the music, eloquent the preacher or profound the prayers. Each worshipper is called to bring their heart to God, and the worship leader is called to help them. This is the devotional dimension of worship.

## Worship as truth-telling or theology

You cannot fool God, and if you are gathering with the intention of encountering the creator of heaven and earth, now is not the time to be economical with the truth. We need to be honest with God about our own desires and actions and, even more, we need to speak the truth about who God is and what God is like. This is what we mean by theology – talking the truth about God. When this is done in a reflective way we call it 'theology', and when we do it in worship we usually call it 'proclamation'. In worship, the Christian community makes explicit what it believes – and especially what it believes about God.

If we were to draw a diagram with arrows indicating who we are addressing in worship, we would find that the arrows point in all sorts of directions. We obviously address God in prayer and praise, in confession, thanksgiving and request. But we also address one another, as the preacher addresses the congregation and, in many of the songs we sing, we speak to each other. A good example is 'Brother, sister, let me serve you'. But sometimes we address ourselves, reminding ourselves of things that are true or of actions we should undertake: 'Praise, my soul, the king of heaven'. Finally, there are times when we announce things to the world in general, what we might call 'public truth', when we attempt to speak the truth to a world which often ignores, avoids, or even seeks to corrupt it. So we speak out about God's goodness and love in a world that desperately needs both, we proclaim forgiveness and reconciliation to a world which is divided, and we name injustices in the interests of God's kingdom.

In all these different directions in which our words are addressed, we are called to speak the truth about God and God's kingdom. In our prayers, we pray in the name, or in the spirit, of Jesus Christ, and this means that the things we say or ask for need to be in character with what we have been shown of Jesus Christ in Scripture. When we give thanks, we are implicitly naming God as the giver of all good things, and when we ask his forgiveness, we are acknowledging that he is a forgiving and gracious God. This is theology – telling the truth about God – and it is a vital part of Christian worship.

This dimension of worship is one which the worship leader must keep clearly in view. Positively, to see worship as an event in which we speak the truth about God is to see it as an event in which we not only speak the truth, but in which we learn the truth. As we shall see in a moment, worship can be very influential in the development of Christians. So, conversely, if the things we say – or imply – about God are not true, then it is a very dangerous matter for the spiritual health of the church. This is one reason why worship leaders and preachers need to be accountable. And this is why the Bible is so important as the basis for the things we say and do in worship, as well as in life.

There are obvious places where we speak about God in worship, such as the sermon. But we also speak about God in the language of prayer and the things we pray for. So what kind of God do we project when we pray? Is it someone concerned about the needs of a broken world, or only someone concerned about our 'spiritual' feelings? Do we imply that God is always asking us to 'try harder', or is God gracious and encouraging, welcoming and inclusive? There is important truth-telling in such implications.

Similarly, congregations have often found that they have learned much truth about God through the hymns they have sung. Especially in churches which have not usually recited creeds, it is in the hymns that the congregation has sung out about the goodness of God, the salvation story of Jesus, his birth, death and resurrection, and has celebrated the forgiveness of sins. The challenge for the worship leader is to select a balanced diet of hymns and songs, so that not only does the congregation have opportunity to express its devotion to God, but also proclaims the goodness and grace of God. As we explored in Chapter 10, it has often been argued that hymns, with their progression of thought, offer better opportunity for theological truth-telling than songs, with their focus on intensifying the moment. You may agree or disagree with this – but what is important is that the things which you ask the congregation to sing provide a balanced diet – a menu of devotional intensity and expansive proclamation of God's grace. Perhaps now you can see how the worship is indeed multi-dimensional, and how this has practical implications for the worship leader.

---

### Exercise

In Chapter 9 I suggested you reflect on the style of prayers that are commonly used in your church, in Chapter 11 on the hymns and songs that have been sung over a four-week period and in Chapter 12 that you survey what Bible readings have been used. Look back on what you discovered in these three exercises. In the light of what has been suggested in this chapter so far, look at the way they come together to make worship as theology.

---

### Worship as formation

We have seen how in worship we not only speak the truth, but learn the truth as well. The things which are said – whether aloud, or by implication, or through our body language – have an effect on the worshippers. Here, in worship, we learn about God and what it means to trust God. In worship, Christians have an opportunity to become more Christian, and the church has an opportunity to become more truly itself. In speaking the truth we give ourselves the possibility of growing into that truth, whether it is the truth of forgiveness, or hope, or whatever.

Rather like a potter shaping and forming the clay into a jar or a bowl, so worship can help shape us into the likeness of Jesus Christ. Of course, this is ultimately the work of God, but our planning worship in a way which recognizes this potential gives God more scope in which to work the miracle of our growth in grace.

It is important to see the Christian life as not only what comes after our conversion or turning to Christ, but as a journey in which we develop and grow, or a process in which we are shaped and formed in

God's image. There are two particular pictures which I think can help us understand this.

First, there is the picture of patterning, where what we do in worship week after week has the effect of impressing upon us certain attitudes and ways of thinking. So when we give thanks, we are not only transacting something – responding to God's generosity – we are also being shaped as people who are grateful and who see in the world evidence of God's generosity. When we praise, we are not only telling God how wonderful he is, we are forming ourselves as people who see the world as being under God's sovereignty. When we bring an offering, or share the peace, our relationship to God is shaped as one of commitment, and our relationship to one another is configured as a relationship of brothers and sisters who are reconciled in Christ.

The second picture is of worship as rehearsal. As we have saw in Chapter 5, worship is a place where we can practise or rehearse being Christians in preparation for being Christians out in the world. It's a bit like practising swimming in the safe context of a swimming pool before we try swimming for real in the ocean. It is hard forgiving in an unforgiving world – so seeking God's forgiveness for ourselves, and forgiving one another before we share bread and wine, are important ways in which we can practise first. To give my testimony to what God has done in my life is hard even in front of fellow Christians – but to do it there is good preparation for testifying to God's goodness in front of unbelievers.

Special mention should be given here to prayer, for it is largely in worship that many Christians learn to pray. From the examples of others leading in extempore prayer, to the carefully crafted words of written or long-used, ancient prayers, we learn what to say and how to say it. This doesn't mean that our own prayers become second hand, a repetition of words we have heard others use. But we learn most things first through copying others and then, with growing confidence, we find our own voices. Just as we copied letters and words when we learned to write, and then eventually could compose our own writings, so we learn to pray through praying with others, and using other's words. Then we can pray from our own hearts – whether using other people's words or our own.

## Worship as pastoral care

The pastoral care of individuals and the local community of Christians is an important dimension of worship, but to understand this clearly we need to think for a moment about what we mean by 'pastoral care'. The phrase may conjure up in your mind the visiting of the sick or the counselling of the troubled. Each of these activities represents an important aspect of what will happen in a ministry of pastoral care, but they have one thing in common: they are both reactive, responding to, and caring for people who need help. Pastoral care is bigger than this, and needs to include a preventative dimension or, more positively still, activities which will result in healthy Christians and healthy churches. This is where worship can play its part.

Pastoral care should include the proactive encouraging of people to grow towards Christian maturity, as well as being a response to human need. The apostle Paul describes the purpose of God's gift of evangelists, pastors and teachers to the Church:

> to equip the saints for the work of ministry, for building up the body of Christ, until all of us come to the unity of the faith and of the knowledge of the Son of God, to maturity, to the measure of the full stature of Christ.
>
> (Ephesians 4.12–13)

We can describe much of this as the work of Christian formation, and it is important to see the overlap between what we might mean by formation and what we might mean by pastoral care. The shepherd doesn't only protect the sheep or bind up their wounds when injured. The shepherd also leads the sheep to good pasture and ensures that they are fed and watered. Healthy worship is nutritionally important in Christian growth. The focus on God and God's grace, learning to pray and learning to listen to Scripture, the celebrating of kingdom values, the developing of a relationship of hope and trust in God, the practising of mutual forgiveness and the sharing of peace – all these are important ways of caring pastorally for the congregation as a whole, as well as its individual members. Over a period of time, it will be important that the worship of a local church embraces a range of biblical material and themes, and that the scope of that worship reaches the different needs of the different members of the congregation. This is where following the Christian year, or the careful selection of a sermon series, can be so important in the provision of a balanced diet.

But we must not ignore that second, responsive aspect of pastoral care – the helping of people in need. Much of this care will happen in a one-to-one way, where people with particular caring gifts and experience will offer help to individuals. However, we must not underestimate the power of worship itself to be used by God in addressing the dire circumstances of some people. It will not be the whole answer, but it can be a part of the way in which God's love will take specific form in the specific circumstances of people's needs.

Yes, the bereaved person will need the comfort and companionship of others who have walked through the valley of the shadow of death – but a focus in worship on the resurrection hope, and a reminder of God's faithful presence in times of trouble will help. Even the singing of hymns – or, more likely, the silent standing while those around sing on our behalf of God's faithfulness – can help mediate the reality that nothing can separate us from God's love.

Yes, the person with low self esteem will need continual encouragement, friendship and affirmation. But a persistent announcing in worship of God's undeserved love to each one of us, and his accepting of us without precondition, will help to build a foundation of grace upon which a new understanding of our value to God can be built.

Yes, the person who is tied in knots by a sense of personal guilt may well need counselling and even confession and absolution. But the preaching of a gospel of grace and the sensitive leading of prayers for forgiveness can help.

Yes, the person hovering on the threshold of Christian faith may well need a friend to help them cross that risky place of trust and commitment. But the continual announcing in worship of God's love and the repeated invitation to follow Jesus may well play their part.

All these are examples of pastoral care in action. It is no surprise that in most churches the pastor is entrusted with the leading of worship, or at least with the oversight of that leading. Care for the Christian community as a whole and care for individual members within it, are closely linked to the worship in which that same community meets regularly in the name of Jesus Christ – that 'great shepherd of the sheep' – in order to express its faith.

---

### Exercise

Think about a number of individuals who might be present next Sunday when your church meets for worship. What have been the significant events in their lives, especially recently? What in worship might help them in their journey and what might hinder them?

---

## Worship as mission

We saw at the beginning of this chapter that we should not see worship as a means to an end. This is particularly important when we consider the way in which worship might help people come to faith. Because worship is an event in which we proclaim the love of God and all he has done for our salvation through Jesus Christ, it is to be expected that worship will be a significant factor in helping people come to faith. Indeed, many Christians look back on particular services as the place where 'the penny dropped' and they saw the world differently, or where they first responded to God in commitment and trust.

This has meant that parts of world Christianity have long seen worship as an important aspect of evangelism. For example, large evangelistic rallies have included worship, and many weekly worship services in local churches have included not only a presentation of the gospel message, but the opportunity for people to respond in faith during the service. This is natural, for in worship we are most explicit about who God is, and how much God loves us – and in worship we are encouraged to act on our faith, trusting in the grace of God.

But there are two further ways in which we need to see the relationship of worship to evangelism. The first concerns the culture of worship. Recent studies of how people come to faith have underlined the importance of relationships, and the way in which people seem to become a part of the Christian community, even before they have made a specific faith commitment. They are drawn to the fellowship, and perhaps spend a period participating in worship as seekers, who are not so much held by their faith as by their questions and the welcoming community of the church. This means that worship leaders need to think carefully about the culture of the worship they lead. Does it include many jargon words that an outsider will not understand? Does it use hymns and songs which are difficult to understand? Different people will come to different views on these questions, but what is important is that they are thought through, both with a concern for the healthy worship of the church and the needs of those on the edge of the church.

Some will be very concerned to provide 'seeker sensitive' worship, in the hope that this will draw more visitors and enable those from an un-churched background to participate and eventually come to faith. This might involve a very informal style of worship and largely consist of presentations from the front, with little singing or other opportunities for congregational participation which might 'threaten' a visitor. Others will argue that to 'water down', as they see it, the worship of the church is not going to help those who are genuinely seeking an encounter with God. Again, what is important is that you think through, and pray through, these issues and, in partnership with others, plan and lead worship accordingly.

Second, an important connection between worship and evangelism comes at the very end of the service, when the congregation is commissioned, sent out and blessed. What signals are worship leaders gong to give out at this point? Are they going to imply that the Christian duty of the congregation is now complete for another week, or are they going to help the congregation to recognize their calling to go out into God's world as witnesses to Jesus Christ? The gathering for worship is to meet God and seek God's kingdom. But part of that seeking of the kingdom is to be sent back into a world which needs to see the kingdom in the lives of the congregation: in caring for the loveless, in championing the marginalized and embracing the outcasts. And this leads us to the last of the dimensions of worship which we can reflect on here – worship and the world.

## Worldly worship

Sometimes, when I am discussing with a group of people about how to define worship (see Chapter 3), it will not be long before someone comments, 'But isn't the whole of life worship?' Of course they are right: every day of our lives should be offered to God and every activity should be an opportunity to glorify God and embody the values of the kingdom. This is what discipleship, following Jesus Christ, is largely about. The apostle Paul made this very point when he wrote to the Romans:

> I appeal to you therefore, brothers and sisters, by the mercies of God, to present your bodies as a living sacrifice, holy and acceptable to God, which is your spiritual worship. Do not be conformed to this world, but be transformed by the renewing of your minds, so that you may discern what is the will of God – what is good and acceptable and perfect.
>
> (Romans 12.1–2)

In the rest of the chapter, Paul spells out what this transformed living looks like. It involves Christians living in harmony, it includes persistence in prayer, patience in suffering and blessing, not cursing, those who treat you badly. In other words, living in the big bad world in a Christ-like way is an act of Christian worship. Of course, Paul is speaking metaphorically, because the picture of the Christian life as an offering is an extension of the root meaning of worship, which is to gather and offer God devotion and praise.

<table>
<tr><td>

**Exercise**

Either look at a couple of outlines of services which you have led recently, or put together outlines of services in which you have been a member of the congregation. Try and work out all the ways that the worship leader sought to make a connection between that worship event and the rest of life. Then rework the outlines, adding suggestions of other possibilities.

</td></tr>
</table>

But this leaves an intriguing and important question: what is the connection between our gathering for communal worship and the living of our lives as a continual act of worship? Unfortunately, this question is often ignored, and many people see little connection, if any, between what happens in worship and what God calls them to do in daily living. This is a tragedy, as both the worship is diminished and our witness weakened. Or put another way, when we separate worship and the rest of life, our worship is ghettoized and our living is secularized. When the connections are not made, our worship becomes inward-looking and dysfunctionally cosy, while our daily living continues unaffected by what we have done, discovered or learned in worship.

In Chapter 5, we looked at a picture to help us understand the connection between worship and the rest of life: this was the idea of focus. I suggested that, in the same way that a lens can focus the rays of the sun so that they combine at a single point, in worship we make explicit that which is always true, yet not always clear. We announce that Jesus Christ is Lord, that God is faithful and that we trust in the forgiveness of sins and the eternal triumph of God's love. These are always true, but in the heat of the day we easily forget or compromise. Our regular gather-

ing for worship – on the first day of the week – enables us to regroup, to remind ourselves of what is true, to refocus our lives on God and the kingdom and to begin again. This is why praise and confession are so important. We centre our lives on God who is the heart of all things

and we are released from past failures and sins and enabled to begin again by God's grace. There is a necessary rhythm to our gathering regularly, because we regularly get it wrong.

What our worship will not normally focus on is what we might think of as abstract theology. However, what we believe about God has very practical implications for our understanding of, and care for 'creation'. Also, it is important that our concerns about the world, and our faithful living in it, are brought into worship, as it is important that our conviction that the world is God's is in turn taken from worship into our daily lives. I call this 'worldly worship', and it impacts on our understanding of worship in a number of ways.

First, we need to recognize that when we gather for worship we should bring the world with us. This is often actively discouraged! We hear prayers like, 'Lord, help us to leave the world behind, to forget our cares and to focus on you'. I understand the sentiment, but I believe it to be mistaken. Jesus encouraged his followers to come to their heavenly father and to ask for things, like children asking a parent. We shouldn't try to repress our anxieties, we should bring them to God in our worship. When we are puzzled by the world, we can offer prayers of lament. When we are concerned about how the world

> 'When we are puzzled by the world we can offer prayers of lament, when we are concerned about how the world is we should not try to forget it, but pray for it. When we get things wrong, we shouldn't bury the evidence but confess our sins.'

is, we should not try to forget it, but pray for it. When we get things wrong, we shouldn't bury the evidence but confess our sins. Worship can express our attempts to live with one another in Christian harmony as the body of Christ, and when we do this we are enacting our hope for the world. This is why the sharing of peace is so potent a sign. Similarly, when someone shares their testimony to God's goodness in their lives, they are reminding us of how the world is the place where God's faithfulness is made known.

When someone proclaims the gospel of Jesus Christ, and another responds in faith by becoming a Christian, the act is not only about worship, but the offering of the whole of their lives. So baptism points to the whole of life as a life to be immersed in God, and both baptism and communion make connections between worship and the world by the use of material things to mediate God's grace – water, bread and wine.

Second, when we worship, we worship a worldly God. This statement isn't as shocking as it might at first seem. After all, the world has been made by God and pronounced good, even though it has been affected by sin. John 3.16 tells us that the spring for God's action in sending Jesus was not out of love for something religious, but 'God so loved the world that he gave his only son . . . '. Time and again the Scriptures testify to God acting in history: calling Abraham, releasing the Hebrew slaves, returning the exiles to the promised land and, ultimately, sending Jesus. The world is the place where God does things, and worship should send us out in anticipation of God's continuing saving work in our world. Indeed, one of the central doctrines of the Christian Church is the doctrine of the incarnation – the belief that God took human flesh and became a part of the world, so that through the life or Jesus Christ, and through his cross and resurrection, the world might be transformed. In Jesus' life we do not see him keeping himself aloof from the troubles of the world, but quite the opposite. He reached out to the outcast, healed broken lives and was criticized by religious people for spending time in bad company.

Much of this can be expressed in terms of the kingdom of God. If our worship is a genuine seeking after God, then we will want what God wants. And that means the transforming of lives and situations in line with what he has revealed in Jesus. To find God in worship is not to escape the world, but to engage with the God who is intimately concerned for the world. So a genuine meeting with God is inevitably going to prepare us for living in God's world. Devotion to Jesus is going to involve our faithful following in places of injustice, amidst the debris of broken relationships and in situations that some call hopeless. This is what it means to talk about celebrating the gospel – to see the world through God's eyes, with love and hope, and to bring that world to God in prayer and trust. This is living worship and worshipful living.

---

### Exercise

Try to remember one or two occasions when your relationship with God was significantly advanced through something which happened in worship. Can you draw any conclusion from this as to how people might be helped to grow in their love of God through particular aspects of worship or ways of leading worship?

---

# 19

# A glossary of grace: the language of worship

I will show my age now and reminisce about the debates which, when I was a teenager, surrounded the publication of new translations of the Bible. Before 1960, most people and churches used the Authorized Version ('King James' to some), though a few used the RSV or Revised Standard Version. Then came the New English Bible, J.B. Phillips' translation of the New Testament, together with other individual translations by Moffatt or Barclay, and eventually the Good News Bible, the New International Version, the New Revised Standard Version, The Message and others. The reason I have wandered down this memory lane is not to debate the relative merits of one translation over against another, but to reflect on a cultural revolution which came in the wake of these translations. Up until the 1960s, the language of the AV was also the language of worship in most congregations. In particular, God was addressed as 'Thee' or 'Thou', and to use 'You' was seen as lacking in respect. With this archaic address there came 'the language of Zion', where biblical quotations and biblical allusions littered every prayer. It was only in the late 1960s that contemporary English began to be used widely in prayers. Before that, it was assumed that there was a special language for worship, which denoted reverence for the holiness of God, a language which was archaic in nature and distinct from the language of every day.

Changes were afoot which were influenced by the revolution in Bible translations, but also by an increasing concern for relevance in worship and communication. The 1960s and '70s were a time when liturgical churches wrote new prayer books, while in many congregations of a more free church and evangelical persuasion, sincerity seemed to be demonstrated by a commitment to the culture of informality which was developing in society a large. The language of prayers was seen to be sincere if it was spontaneous and even hesitant, down-to-earth rather than rhetorical.

We can now see that this shift, while well intentioned, was a correcting swing of the pendulum against a previously ponderous style of worship. But such cultural pendulums, by their very nature, tend to swing too far and it's clear that there does need to be a special language for worship. This is not something which is artificially reverent, but which grows out of a genuine attempt to give God due reverence and recognizes that there are things too deep to be put into everyday words.

This language of worship has, for me, two dimensions. First there is the way in which special words and evocative phrases help communicate realities which are not easily expressed in the same turns of phrase we might use while shopping or discussing sport. It reminds me that many different kinds of activities require the use of a specialist language or rhetoric, and worship need be no different in this. And second, there are the words themselves – what some might regard as jargon, but which I want to call 'a glossary of grace'.

## Stretching words: the language of worship

Different forms of communication are used for different kinds of activities. The language of an instruction manual for a car will be different from the language of a novel, and the language of the shopping trip will be different from the language a lover uses to express devotion for the beloved.

Some things are easy. We can describe, say, a building, or give instructions that will help a stranger find their way through our town. But how do we express love, and how do we describe how much another person means to us? For this we will use metaphor and even poetry, and it will be a common experience to discover that the words are quite inadequate to express how we truly feel.

If this is true for human relationships, how much more is it going to affect how we speak about God, and how we express our worship and the depths of our feelings and concerns? This is why hymns and songs are so important in worship. Not only do they offer the opportunity for singing together, but they tend to be written in poetic form. The plain language of explanation is very important in communicating certain things and can have its place in worship, such as in some preaching and in the directions that the congregation may be given before doing something new – and, of course, the notices! But even more important will be an evocative language, which attempts to express the inexpressible and leads us beyond our own limited experience to the wonders of God's love, revealed in Scripture and the lives and experience of other Christians.

Do not be discouraged: not all of us are poets or even wordsmiths. But we are called to point people to realities too deep for words. The great Christian writer John Bunyan said that,

> The best prayers have often more groans than words; and those words that it hath, are but a lean and shallow representation of the heart, life, and spirit of that Prayer.

This may well be true in personal devotion, but in corporate worship the leader needs to help the whole congregation to pray and so will need to develop strategies to help in this calling. This may mean using prayers written by others, or words of Scripture, or periods of silence with a few prompts. Often it will be a combination of these ways, together with spontaneous, heartfelt prayer. What is important is that we recognize the challenge of talking about God in words which were really designed for more mundane purposes.

A young man was once dancing in the aisle of his church during worship and one of the more traditional members of the congregation challenged him by asking him why he thought he needed to dance. He answered, 'Because I can't fly!' In worship, we have to do the best we can with what we have got. Words will always let us down, but we need to use them as best we can, supplementing them, of course, with other forms of expression, such as musical and visual expression.

Of course it's beyond me – that's why we worship:

> I pray that you may have the power to comprehend, with all the saints, what is the breadth and length and height and depth, and to know the love of Christ that surpasses knowledge, so that you may be filled with all the fullness of God.
>
> Now to him who by the power at work within us is able to accomplish abundantly far more than we can ask or imagine, to him be glory in the church and in Christ Jesus to all generations, for ever and ever. Amen.
>
> (Ephesians 3.18–21)

## Grace-filled words: the vocabulary of worship

There are particular words which carry meanings that are not easily expressed in other ways – except by using a lot of words. That's what I have attempted in the remaining section of this chapter – simple explanations of some of these words which are rich in meaning.

The list is incomplete, both in what I say about each, and in those words which I fail to include. This is inevitably a personal list and I hope it will offer you a starting point, encouraging you to reflect more on the rich language of worship which points us to the abundant grace of God that is beyond words.

Sometimes I will use one of these words because it is the best way of expressing a particular truth about God, or our relationship with God, that I want to communicate. But I also recognize that the word will not be understood by everyone, and so I will add a phrase or a sentence in order to hint at the meaning I have in mind. It is important not to labour such explanations, but simply to suggest where the grace-filled word is pointing in our exploration of God.

Here are some examples of how we might use meaning-full words, while also explaining them without labouring the issue:

We are a covenant people: God has called us into relationship with him and with one another.

We are able to worship God because of the grace of God: we stand here not because of our own goodness but because God loves us, has forgiven us and invites us into fellowship.

We come in adoration: giving God our undivided attention, we come in love and praise.

## Glossary

**Adoration** is the praise of a lover. It will be reverent, but it will include affection as well as respect, and will often be expressed with gentleness. Think of the mood of, 'Father, I adore you, lay my life before you. How I love you.' In worship it may come at the beginning, but it is more likely to come at moments of devotional intensity, when we are 'lost in wonder, love and praise'.

**Assurance** is a state of confidence in the love and mercy of God. Assurance grows from a realization of God's grace, that we come close to God, not because of our own goodness but because of God's love for us: 'In this is love, not that we loved God but that he loved us and gave his Son to be the atoning sacrifice for our sins' (1 John 4.10).

**Benediction** literally means 'good word' and usually refers to the words of prayer or blessing at the close of a service. These words should send people out with hope in their hearts and the promise that there is nowhere they can go where God is not there with them. The benediction may include words of commissioning for service or witness, but it should always include words of blessing.

**Blessing** can either be in the form of a request to God or a pronouncement on behalf of God. To bless is to seek a fullness of life before God for someone else. At the end of the service, it is the assurance that we do not leave God behind when we leave the place of worship, and that the God who accompanies us is the faithful and gracious God revealed in Jesus Christ and present through the Holy Spirit. Consequently, this final blessing should usually evoke the name of the Trinity: Father, Son and Holy Spirit.

At other places in worship, such as when an individual is prayed for, or commissioned for service, the words of the 'Aaronic Blessing' (Numbers 6.24–26) are often used:

> The Lord bless you and keep you;
> the Lord make his face to shine upon you, and be gracious to you;
> the Lord lift up his countenance upon you, and give you peace.

**Call** is a central theme in the Bible. Abraham was called by God, as were the prophets and, eventually, the disciples who were gathered around Jesus through his ministry and whom he then sent out to make more disciples (Matthew 28.19–20). In worship, the congregation gathers because it is called by God, and the opening of the service should express this in a way that suggests more than simply a sociable welcome. A 'call to worship' will usually involve a very short Bible reading, which either expresses an invitation to worship, such as Psalm 100.4–5,or proclaims some aspect of who God is, and to which the natural reaction is an act of praise.

**Creator** is a common title for God and reminds us that God is the source of all things, the maker of heaven and earth. To acknowledge God as creator carries implications, both for our view of God, and our understanding of the world. To name God as creator is to remind ourselves of the huge gulf between ourselves as creatures and the transcendent and almighty maker of all things. We express this in praise and in the faith that God is able to do all that he promises. He is also the God of **new creation** who has raised Jesus from the dead and offered us new life in Christ.

To name God as 'creator' also implies that we see the natural universe as **creation**, the work of a creator by whom we are entrusted with the responsible stewardship of creation. In worship, this will encourage us to pray for this world and dedicate ourselves to its care and renewal.

The **Cross** is the central visual symbol of Christianity, and many churches will have a representation of the cross at the front of their worship space as a focus for worship and a sign that our gathering for worship is made possible by the work of salvation and reconciliation God achieved in Christ through the cross. Some evangelical Christians insist in using an 'empty' cross as a sign that the cross only has meaning in the light of the resurrection, though for some there will be a suspicion of images which militates against representing an image of Jesus at the focal point of worship.

Others will see in the body of Jesus on the cross a reminder both of his sharing our humanity and of the great sacrifice that lies at the heart of our salvation. Isaac Watts' great hymn, 'When I survey the wondrous cross', evokes some of these themes:

See from His head, His hands, His feet,
Sorrow and love flow mingled down!
Did e'er such love and sorrow meet,
Or thorns compose so rich a crown?

Were the whole realm of nature mine,
That were a present far too small;
Love so amazing, so divine,
Demands my soul, my life, my all.

**Dedication** is the offering of ourselves to someone else for some act of service. It is a central aspect of what it means to be a Christian, for when we say that 'Jesus is Lord' we are not only proclaiming something which is universally true, but we are announcing that he is my Lord. As followers of Jesus Christ, we dedicate ourselves to him and to the service of God and his kingdom. A key biblical text is Romans 12.1–2:

I appeal to you therefore, brothers and sisters, by the mercies of God, to present your bodies as a living sacrifice, holy and acceptable to God, which is your spiritual worship. Do not be conformed to this world, but be transformed by the renewing of your minds, so that you may discern what is the will of God – what is good and acceptable and perfect.

I believe that all worship should contain an element of dedication, and a worship leader should provide suitable opportunities for the members of a congregation to express their personal response to God and God's word. This will include suitable hymns and songs, prayers, times of silence and the opportunity to respond either by going to the front of the worship area or by some other action, such as the lighting of a candle, or the offering of a personal prayer (see Chapter 16).

**Devotion** implies a warmth of affection and a close and loyal attachment to someone. For Christians, it will refer to a dimension in our relationship with God which takes us beyond the duty of a worshipper before a divine being, or the obligations of a subject to their ruler. In the words of an ancient prayer, it is both our duty and our delight to worship God and the devotional aspect of worship will express something of this loving joy and warm affection. Devotion may also express our longing for God, as in Psalm 42.1–2:

As a deer longs for flowing streams, so my soul longs for you, O God. My soul thirsts for God, for the living God.

All worship should express something of this delight in God, as it testifies both to God's love for us and our love for God. Worship songs, with their opportunity for repetition and intensification may be particularly helpful in expressing and encouraging this dimension of worship, but testimony and spontaneity will also play their part.

A **Disciple** is a learner and, in the Christian context, a follower of Jesus Christ. In particular, a disciple learns in the context of his or her relationship to the master, and the centrality of Jesus Christ to our worship is not only a theological necessity, but a means whereby worshippers are formed in his likeness. Dedication is important in this, but so is an openness to the word of God and the work of the Spirit in our lives.

**Exhortation** is the act of encouraging others to act or think in a particular way. It is a vital part of Christian preaching and expresses the belief that God calls us to continued acts of dedication and service. However, it must always be balanced by a strong appreciation of grace: that we do not earn God's love or approval through trying harder. Rather, God's acceptance of us sets us free to respond in service and increased trust and devotion.

**Faith** is another way of speaking about trust. Through faith we are accepted by God, yet this faith is not some act of will on our part but a living trust that God is faithful and that he has set us free from our sins and their consequences. Sometimes people talk about 'the Faith' and mean by it the things which Christians believe – but the fundamental and most important meaning of the word 'faith' is a life of trust in which we depend upon God and all he has done for us in Christ and continues to do through the work of the Holy Spirit. All our worship is based on the reality of our trusting God, and this dependence on divine grace will be a central theme of our prayers and songs, our preaching and final blessing.

**Faithfulness** is closely related to faith. We trust God because God is faithful. His character doesn't change, but is eternally as it is revealed to us in Jesus Christ, who is 'the same, yesterday and today and forever' (Hebrews 13.8). Worship should encourage the worshippers to trust God's faithfulness, but it will also give voice to the testimonies of those who have known that faithfulness in the midst of trouble and dangers.

God calls us to be faithful as well, both in a regular gathering for worship and in our daily witness in the world. Worship should encourage and equip followers of Jesus to be faithful in all circumstances, and thus to re-discover God's faithfulness:

> For I am convinced that neither death, nor life, nor angels, nor rulers, nor things present, nor things to come, nor powers, nor height, nor depth, nor anything else in all creation, will be able to separate us from the love of God in Christ Jesus our Lord.
>
> (Romans 8.38–39)

**Fellowship** expresses the belief that a fundamental aspect of the church community is the communion which binds its members together through the saving work of Jesus Christ and the renewing action of the Holy Spirit. In Scripture, it translates the Greek word *koinonia* which combines a sense of affectionate relationships with a practical sharing of resources. The words of 'the Grace', which are often used in worship ('The grace of the Lord Jesus Christ, the love of God and the fellowship/communion/sharing (*koinonia*) of the Holy Spirit, be with us all'), are a reminder that this fellowship is the work of God who draws us together through the Holy Spirit. It is as we live 'in God' that our relationships are transformed, and we become a foretaste of the unity and reconciliation which will be heaven.

**Forgiveness** is the act of releasing someone from the consequences of an injury they have caused you, and therefore is also an action which leads to reconciliation and the healing of your relationship with them. We are all sinners and in need of God's forgiveness, which has been made possible through the atoning death of Jesus Christ on the cross. Theologians have developed different theories as to how the cross has led to forgiveness, but Christians are agreed that the cross is the focus of God's forgiving and saving action in Christ.

In worship, we confess our sins and seek again God's forgiveness. The gospel of forgiveness enables us to be honest about the state of our lives and realistic in our worship. We do not need to pretend that we are better that we are, and the declaration (or 'assurance') of our forgiveness is a liberating action of great pastoral significance.

God also calls us to be forgiving people, as the Lord's Prayer makes clear, and the sharing of peace at the Lord's Supper is an important sign and expression that Christian community is founded on mutual forgiveness, as well as mutual love.

**Gospel** literally means 'good news'. This good news is not a collection of information but is a person, Jesus Christ. When we preach the gospel we are announcing who Jesus is and what he has done. This gospel proclamation naturally leads to people trusting him for their salvation and becoming his disciples. Because the core of the Christian proclamation is good news, this should influence the tone of all Christian worship. Proclamation leads to celebration, as the announcing of the gospel leads to repentance, faith and joy.

**Grace** is undeserved favour, and for Christians this is a fundamental aspect of what we believe about God (see 'assurance' above). God is gracious, which means he loves us before we love him, and that all we do in response to his love is made possible by the work of the Holy Sprit within us.

Paul indicates that, even when we pray, we are prompted and inspired by the Spirit of God (Romans 8.15–16, 26–27). Like a child who is given pocket money by a parent so that they might buy the parent a birthday present, so God gives us everything we need to truly worship. Before the holy God we have no ground on which to stand other than God's grace.

Like the father in the parable of the two sons (Luke 15.11–32), God comes to meet us on our journey back to him, despite our bad behaviour and even our mixed motives, embracing us and throwing a party. This is grace.

**Healing** is the restoring of that which is sick or broken. It was a central part of the ministry of Jesus and our prayers for healing demonstrate a holistic concern for the whole person, body as well as soul. But there is also a healing of the spirit: 'he leads me beside still waters; he restores my soul' (Psalm 23.2–3). In this, healing is closely related to forgiveness because when we are forgiven we do not only ask to be 'let off' or released from the consequences of our sins; we also ask to be cleansed and renewed, as we are reformed into the likeness of Jesus Christ.

The **Heart** is the centre of the person, the 'heart' of who they are. This is a biblical metaphor for the depths of a person: the seat of their emotions, the focus of their desires and the location of their will. The *Shema* of Deuteronomy 6.4–5, which Jesus identifies as the first of the commandments (Mark 12.29–30), calls us to love God with all our heart, with all our soul and with all our strength.

Unless we worship God with our hearts, we are not truly worshipping, though some people will express this more openly than others. Heart worship, or devotion, should be a central concern of anyone leading others in worship, and opportunity and encouragement should be given for a warmth of devotional worship to take place: adoration and love, commitment and repentance are all aspects of a genuine worship from the heart.

**Holiness** has two meanings, one relating to God and one relating to worshippers. In relation to God, holiness is the 'godness' of God, and reminds us of the gulf between Almighty God and us sinners. When God spoke to Moses out of the burning bush, he told him to remove his sandals as the ground on which he stood was holy ground (Exodus 3.5), and when Isaiah had a vision of God enthroned amidst the cherubim, he heard them calling, 'Holy, holy, holy is the Lord of hosts, the whole earth is full of his glory' (Isaiah 6.3).

A central theme of the Old Testament is the linking of holiness as an attribute of God with an apprehension of God's moral perfection. So holiness came not only to refer to God's transcendence (or God's distance from us by virtue of being our creator), but it came to refer to God's goodness in contrast to our sinfulness. We can only enter into fellowship with this holy God through God's grace, and especially because of our forgiveness through Christ's saving work.

The second meaning of holiness refers to people or things, and denotes that they are dedicated, or set apart, for God. So Christians are called to be holy in their dedication to God and in the kind of lives they live, as in 1 Peter 2.9:

> But you are a chosen race, a royal priesthood, a holy nation, God's own people, in order that you may proclaim the mighty acts of him who called you out of darkness into his marvellous light.

**Hope** is a central theme of the New Testament and consists of a confidence in the future. This is not based on a superficial optimism or a belief in our own abilities, but on the promises of God and a belief that God is both willing and able to fulfil those promises. Our hope for the future is based on God and what has been revealed in Jesus Christ. So when we celebrate as in Philippians that 'every tongue should confess that Jesus Christ is Lord, to the glory of God the Father', we are celebrating what one hymn proclaims as 'love is on the throne'. The future is 'Christ-centred', yet something of this is already a present reality, as 'hope does not disappoint us, because God's love has been poured into our hearts through the Holy Spirit that has been given to us' (Romans 5.5).

**Intercession** is praying for others. It is an act of love in which we bring the needs of the world and the needs of those we care for to God. Worship which lacks intercession is in danger of being inward-looking and selfish. Interceding for the needs of the world is an important way of seeking the kingdom of God and of expressing the missionary love for the world for which Christ died (John 3.16).

**Invitation** is not an especially religious term, but it does represent an important aspect of worship. We are invited to gather for worship (see 'call' above) by the God who loves us and seeks to draw us close. The kingdom which Jesus proclaims has an open-door policy (see Luke 14.15–24), and our worship should be welcoming and inclusive, both in its message and in its practical arrangements for welcoming guests and strangers.

**Justice** is an important theme in Scripture and a part of the nature of God. There are such things as right and wrong, and God calls us not only to be believers, but to 'do the right':

He has told you, O mortal, what is good;
and what does the Lord require of you
but to do justice, and to love kindness
and to walk humbly with your God?

(Micah 6.8)

Justice insists that we treat our fellow human beings well, and calls us to be good stewards of the gifts of creation with which we are entrusted. Scripture presents God as the judge of all the earth, and we live and worship in the knowledge that all will be revealed before him. Again, it is only through grace and the forgiveness of God that we who live in injustice can hope to stand before the judge of all, and this tension between judgement and acceptance should permeate all our worship.

The **Kingdom of God** was a central theme of the teaching of Jesus. To speak of God's rule is to proclaim a state of affairs where God's will is done 'on earth as it is in heaven', and prayer for this rule of God is a key part of the Lord's Prayer. The kingdom is both 'now and not yet', as God is Lord of all, and yet not all acknowledge that Lordship. God's will is done in situations and lives here and now, yet God's complete will will not be fulfilled until the end of time. So Christians are called to live that future rule of God even now in a world which does not recognize him, and this leads to trouble and persecution. It is no wonder that we pray:

Your kingdom come.
  Your will be done,
    on earth as it is in heaven . . .
And do not bring us to the time of trial,
  but rescue us from the evil one.

(Matthew 6.10, 13)

**Life** is a gift of God. God 'knit me together in my mother's womb' (Psalm 139.13), and I live my life in the knowledge that it is a gift to be enjoyed and a gift to be returned to the Giver. Life is more than mere existence, and in Jesus Christ we encounter the One who is 'the way, the truth and life itself' (John 14.6). This theme of life should encourage us to offer lively worship in which we celebrate God's gifts.

**Love** is the heart of God: 'Whoever does not love does not know God, for God is love' (1 John 4.8). When Paul writes (1 Corinthians 13.8) of the three most important things – faith, hope and love – he indicates that only love is eternal. When we are face to face with God we will no longer need faith and when God's purposes are accomplished, we will no longer need hope. But always there will be love – for God is love.

With such a vision we must ensure that love is the golden thread running through all our worship: God's love for us, and God's love for the world; the love which the Holy Spirit kindles within us, and the love which binds Christians together into the body of Christ. Paul prays that his readers might 'know the love of Christ which is beyond knowing' so that they 'may be filled with the fullness of God' (Ephesians 3.19). Such a vision draws us into worship which is full of 'wonder, love and praise'.

**Mission** is a sending with a purpose. We may talk about 'the mission of the church', and express it in worship by commissioning the congregation to go out in witness and service, but we must always remember that, in truth, the mission is God's. It is not that we work on behalf of God: rather, we make ourselves available for God to work through us. This means that the dedication of our lives which we make in worship is far wider than simply a devotional offering of our hearts to God, it is a giving of the whole of our lives in all their practical dealings.

Worship which focuses on mission will proclaim the love and faithfulness of God. It will both offer an invitation for worshippers to put their trust in God, and it will call them to share God's love with others. It will be a worship open to the world in which we pray, 'Your kingdom come, your will be done, on earth as it is in heaven.'

**Obedience** is not a comfortable word for many Western Christians who are more used to the cult of the individual and a culture in which consumer choice is a supreme value. Yet if we affirm the Lordship of Christ, we must also speak of obedience to the rule of Christ. If we truly worship God, then we must be open 'to do and bear' his holy will for our lives. The language of obedience and submission to the will of God is counter-cultural, yet we must be open to what God wants to do through us and what God wants to do in us. Then we will discover God's service is 'perfect freedom'.

**Peace** is God's will for all creation. The Old Testament word is *shalom*, and this peace is not simply the absence of hostilities, but the presence of justice and wholeness. In the New Testament, peace marks the relationship one Christian should have with another and is both the work of the Holy Spirit and something we should strive for (Ephesians 4.3). The gospel is a gospel of reconciliation, and peace is the fruit of such reconciling work.

In worship we may share the peace, particularly during the Lord's Supper, as an expression of reconciliation made possible by the cross of Christ. But at all times we should see the worshipping community as a company of people called to live and witness to God's peace. This is why disagreement about worship is particularly dangerous. What is the point of winning a battle of wills over the style of worship, if my victory testifies to my argumentative spirit rather than the reconciling work of Christ, or the peace which is the fruit of the Holy Spirit?

**Petition** is a prayer of request and usually refers to prayers for ourselves. Sometimes people think that is a lower kind of prayer than adoration or contemplation, but this is not true. When Jesus taught about prayer, he encouraged us to come before God as children bringing requests to their father:

> Ask, and it will be given you; search, and you will find; knock, and the door will be opened for you. For everyone who asks receives, and everyone who searches finds, and for everyone who knocks, the door will be opened.
>
> (Matthew 7.7–8)

When we bring our requests to God, we are demonstrating our trust in God and our belief in his faithfulness. However, we must also pray for others, as this is a sign of the love which God wishes to grow in our hearts.

**Power** is a difficult word because it can have both positive and negative meanings. If power is misused, then people are manipulated or coerced in ways which contradict the way of love.

God is a God of power, but his power is shown in weakness, both the weakness of the cross (1 Corinthians 1.22–25) and our own experience of weakness as followers of Jesus (2 Corinthians 4.7). Yet, in worship, we call on God to empower us for service, enabling us to be used by the Holy Spirit for witnessing to Jesus and doing and living his will.

**Praise** is, arguably, the core activity of worship, for in the act of praise we acknowledge and proclaim who God is. We give honour to the only One in the universe worthy of our worship, and name God as the only Lord of all. Although they often intertwine in worship, it is helpful to distinguish between praise and thanksgiving. In thanksgiving we honour God for what he has done or given – and in praise we honour God for who God is.

Praise will usually occur early in a worship service, though it is appropriate at any time. In praise we announce the character of God, and place God at the centre of our attention and at the heart of our allegiance. In this, words will often fail us and we will need to break into song or silence:

> Praise the LORD, all you nations!
>   Extol him, all you peoples!
> For great is his steadfast love towards us,
>   and the faithfulness of the Lord endures for ever.
> Praise the LORD!
>
> (Psalm 117)

**Prayer** is the dominant mode of worship, for in prayer we address God and open ourselves to the work of the Holy Spirit. Prayer may be spoken or silent; it may be extempore, pre-composed or read from a book; it may be sung as a hymn, opened up for congregational free prayer or said responsively. Whichever of these methods apply, it should always be a prayer of the heart, where the worshippers make themselves vulnerable before our gracious and loving God. In worship, we can learn to pray through the words and example of others, and through our own paying attention in mind and heart to God, who both listens to and inspires our prayer.

**Proclamation** is the announcing of what is true – especially about God and the gospel of Jesus Christ. The sermon should, in this sense, be proclamation, but we also proclaim in the hymns and songs we sing, the Scriptures we read and many of the other things which we do in worship (see Chapter 18). What we believe about God is good news and we cannot keep it to ourselves. The result is proclamation.

**Reconciliation** is the act of bringing together those who have been estranged. So we are brought close to God through the atoning death of Christ on the cross, and through the Holy Sprit we are reconciled with those from whom our sin had separated us (2 Corinthians 5.17–19; Ephesians 2.11–14). Peace and communion are the result of reconciliation, and this is supremely expressed in the Lord's Supper where our unity with one another is expressed through our sharing of bread and wine, the signs of Christ's reconciling cross.

The **Resurrection** of Jesus was a world-changing event in which God reversed the judgement of the cross and said 'Amen!' to all that Jesus had said and done. Through the lens of the resurrection we see our own eternal destiny and we celebrate that nothing can separate us from God's love, not even death. All our worship is undertaken in the light of the resurrection, for Jesus is alive and as we gather in his name we do so trusting in his promise, 'Where two or three are gathered in my name, I am there among them' (Matthew 18.20).

**Sustainer** is a word we can use about God who sustains the universe in existence and supports us in times of difficulty. God is faithful, and it is often in tough times and tough situations we discover that, as we try to hold on to God, God is holding on to us.

**Thanksgiving** is a central part of worship. In giving thanks, we not only thank God for his generosity and grace, but we learn to see the world differently. When we give thanks, we see the world as a gift of God and our lives as a sign of God's generosity; we learn that we are stewards of God's gifts and that we are called to live lives of generosity.

**Trust** is a basic requirement for wholesome living. We learn that anyone can let us down, and only God is the one in whom we can truly trust. In worship we express our trust in God and are encouraged to trust him even more.

**Unity** is the fruit of reconciliation. In worship, we come to God and all barriers between believers should be set aside. In reality, this is not often our experience, and we need to seek God's forgiveness and help. In worship we should anticipate and rehearse the unity in Christ which God desires for all humanity. Worship is a communal activity, but the congregation is not a social group which comes together because of social kinship or because of intellectual agreement. The congregation is formed because of unity in Christ, who is the Saviour and Lord of all.

---

### Exercise

Add other words to this list, either because you think they are important or because you are unsure exactly what they mean. If necessary find someone to ask about the meaning where it is unclear.

---

# 20

# Continuing the journey

By the time you have reached this point in the book, you might feel you want to collapse in a heap, and that any more talk of journeys will just increase your exhaustion! When you begin any new type of activity, there will be times when you feel overwhelmed. Learning to lead worship is no exception.

In truth, there is no simple formula that I can give you which will guarantee success – whatever that means. You need to learn, to practise, to reflect on how things have gone, adjust your practice, try again, reflect again, and so on. This is the only way to develop in anything which is worthwhile. And what can be more worthwhile than the worship of God?

This book has frequently used the image of a journey to talk about the progression of a worship event. But we could also use the image of a journey to talk about your progression as a worship leader. Sometimes the terrain will be tough, and sometimes your energy levels will be low, but the journey is worth it. Sometimes you may be tempted to give up, and sometimes you may feel you have lost your way, but the journey is worth it.

It is good to go on a journey with others. Travelling companions can encourage and guide us. Worship itself is a communal activity, and learning to lead will be helped by the companionship of others. Learn from others: imitate people you respect, though never try to be other than yourself. Seek advice and constructive criticism from people you can trust. And remind yourself that you should never stop learning.

But how do we evaluate our progress? How do we make judgements about what is good, and not so good, practice? In other words, what does it mean to talk about 'quality' in relation to worship and in our own contributions to it?

## A question of quality

The outgoing music drifts on the breeze and the preacher stands at the door waiting to shake hands with the energized witnesses who are about to take the world by storm. 'Thank you for your message' and 'I did enjoy that' are often the best feedback they can muster.

There's a hush in the church meeting as the matter of repairs to the organ is raised. The arguments are marshalled: 'What we want is relevant worship – quality communication for the twenty-first century! Don't waste money on the organ.' Others argue, 'We want to give God our best! That means the treasures of great music, not Radio 2 jingles over and over again . . . '. And so the battle lines are drawn. Everyone wants the best – it's just they can't agree what the best looks like.

Many areas of life now have to face up to issues of quality assurance, especially in the public sector. We justifiably want the best possible health service, the best possible schools and universities – the best possible customer satisfaction. But what might quality assurance mean for worship? What is the sliding scale from weak to strong or from great to awful? How are we to judge what is the best?

When a choir sings to lead worship is there a place for the tone deaf in its ranks? Does 'best' mean the best possible sound quality – or does 'best' mean an inclusive hospitality that works with all those who want to be a part of the praise?

Does the 'best' music mean the best as in 'classically sublime', or the best as in 'culturally relevant'? Does it mean the best for attracting visitors, or the best for helping a particular congregation to worship? And what does the 'best' preaching mean, or the 'best' prayers?

The danger is that we choose our quality standards on the basis of our personal preferences, and then claim them to be some kind of objective benchmark. So here are two suggestions for assessing the quality of our worship.

First, judge the activity by assessing how far it enables the purposes of worship to be achieved – meeting God and seeking God's kingdom. So after a worship event we can ask, 'Has this service enabled the congregation to meet the living God?' and 'Have we been enabled to seek the things which God wants?' The questions not only raise issues of technique and music selection – but challenge as to whether or not the authentic gospel has been proclaimed. Has the living God been allowed to speak through Scripture and silence, through openness to devotion and openness to the world? Quality worship is to be found in truthfulness and sincerity, in love, joy and repentance.

Second, the benchmark of good worship may differ according to the one who judges. With a diverse congregation of young and old, highbrow and lowbrow, traditional and trendy, black and white, the standards of quality may differ wildly. When this happens, one mark of quality will be whether the worship has enabled fellowship, whether it has built up the body of Christ in its rich diversity.

Who judges what is good? Is it the visitor who is welcomed or ignored, is it the child who is celebrated or shushed, is it the musician who feels fulfilled or the pensioner who can't cope with the noise?

And what if the one judging the quality of worship is actually God? After all, it is supposed to be the worship of God. And how do we avoid projecting our wish list on to the living God? This is why worship needs to be grounded in Scripture. We need to rejoice and weep with the psalmist, to be open to the Spirit with the early Church, to listen to the prophets and to walk with Jesus.

Here are some quality starting points from Scripture:

Let us test and examine our ways, and return to the LORD.
Let us lift up our hearts as well as our hands to God in heaven.

(Lamentations 3.40–41)

and

He has told you, O mortal, what is good; and what does the LORD require of you but to do justice, and to love kindness, and to walk humbly with your God?

(Micah 6.8)

A worship leader is called to help a particular congregation, on a particular day and in a particular place, to worship God. We are called to give our best – but the best is what will best help this congregation give of its best to God – who is the best. We will want to make technical judgements about the quality of the music or the preaching (we would never improve otherwise), but we will also do all our judging in the light of God who is gracious and loving. If we are judging ourselves, we need to do it in the light of God's grace and calling of us. If we are judging the performance of others, we need to do it gently and in love.

I was once given good advice on commenting on the manner of someone else leading worship. If you have positive things to say then say them after the service. If you have 'constructive criticism' to offer, then 'wait 'til Wednesday'! Immediately after the service, a leader will be most vulnerable to negative feedback, so wait until you can be measured and gentle, and until they can hear and receive what you have to say without being hurt or defensive.

## Approaching God

And so we reach the end of this book – apart from the suggestions for further reading and the list of possible worship resources. I wish you well as you seek to serve God and his people through the leading of worship, or as you seek to deepen your own understanding of worship.

Remember – it's all about God. This book is called *Approaching God* because it is about Christians gathering in order to meet God in worship. We are approaching God through Scripture, prayer and praise. Whatever else might be happening, this is our core concern: to approach God as sincere worshippers, with open hearts and dedicated lives.

But this book is also called *Approaching God* because the God we worship is the God who approaches us, coming in grace and love to delight in our presence, to forgive our sins and transform our lives.

We have seen how the themes of the Christian year centre our attention on God's work in Jesus Christ, but there is also a sense in which the themes remind us that the God we worship is the God who comes to meet us. In Advent, we celebrate the God who comes – coming in covenant promise in the Old Testament and in the preparation for the coming of Jesus Christ. At Christmas, God comes as Immanuel – God with us – to share our human existence and transform it. In Holy Week and Easter, God comes even to the limits of our experience – death itself – so that we might share in the risen life of his son. At Pentecost, God comes as the Holy Spirit to transform and renew our lives – to work in us and to work through us. This is our 'Approaching God'.

What good news this is! What an invitation! What grace!

This is the God we worship:
   the God who doesn't wait for us
   but comes looking for his children.
This is the God we worship:
   the one who puts breath in our bodies
   and prayers on our lips.
This is the God we worship:
   the God who doesn't hide
   but approaches us and calls us by name.
This is the God we worship:
   what else can we do but bow down
   and be lifted into the loving embrace.
This is worship.

# 21

# Exploring further

These suggestions for further reading are loosely arranged according to the chapters of this book. But often these books overlap various subjects so I have combined some chapters and sections. There are also subjects, such as the history of worship, which I have not dealt with in this book but which may be of interest to someone wanting to explore further. I have included some books which may already be out of print, because they are really useful and it is often quite simple to order second-hand copies over the internet.

I have grouped all the websites together as they are primarily providers of resources. There does, of course, need to be a health warning about websites. New ones spring up regularly and no doubt some good ones on worship will appear between my writing this book and its being published – let alone your reading it. Similarly, websites end without warning and the ones I include may no longer be operational by the time you try and access them. However, I hope this book will give you enough basics to enable you to use a search engine and find your own sites. Happy hunting!

Of course, I cannot underwrite what you find on the Web – and I do not necessarily agree with all that is written in the books I recommend. But I hope you continue the worship journey and here are a few pointers to get you started.

Books which are particularly useful as an introduction to a subject are marked with an asterisk (*).

## Further reading

### *Beginnings*

J. Vogel and M. Sytsma, *Sunday Morning Live: How and Why We Worship*, Grand Rapids, MI: Faith Alive Christian Resources and Calvin Institute of Christian Worship, 2003

*J. F. White, *Introduction to Christian Worship*, Nashville, TN: Abingdon, 1980

S. J. White, *Groundwork of Christian Worship*, London: Epworth, 1997

## Meanings

C. J. Ellis, *Gathering: A Theology and Spirituality of Worship in Free Church Tradition*, London: SCM Press, 2004
D. B. Forrester, J. I. H. McDonald, and G. Tellini, *Encounter with God: An Introduction to Christian Worship and Practice*, Edinburgh: T & T Clark, 1996
G. Kendrick, *Worship*, Eastbourne: Kingsway Publications, 1984
William Temple, *Readings in St John's Gospel* (new edn), Wilton, CT: Morehouse, 1985
R. E. Webber, *Worship Old and New: A Biblical, Historical and Practical Introduction (Revised)*, Grand Rapids, MI: Zondervan, 1994
R. E. Webber, *Worship is a Verb*, Peabody, MA: Hendrickson, 1996
S. J. White, *The Spirit of Worship: The Liturgical Tradition*, London: Darton, Longman & Todd, 1999

## History of Christian Worship

L. W. Hurtado, *At the Origins of Christian Worship: The Context and Character of Earliest Christian Devotion*, Grand Rapids, MI and Cambridge, UK: Eerdmans, 1999
Ralph P. Martin, *Worship in the Early Church*, London and Edinburgh: Marshall, Morgan and Scott, 1974
*J. F. White, *A Brief History of Christian Worship*, Nashville, TN: Abingdon, 1993
W. H. Willimon, *Word, Water, Wine and Bread: How Worship has Changed over the Years*, Valley Forge, PA: Judson, 1980

## Planning the Journey

B. Berglund, *Reinventing Sunday: Breakthrough Ideas for Transforming Worship*, Valley Forge, PA: Judson, 2001
F. M. Segler and F. M. Bradley, *Understanding, Preparing for and Practicing Christian Worship*, Nashville, TN: Broadman & Holman, 1996

## Praying

Mary Batchelor, *The Lion Prayer Collection: Over 1330 Prayers for All Occasions*, Oxford: Lion Hudson, 1996
Emily R. Brink, John D. Witvliet and others, *The Worship Sourcebook*, Grand Rapids, MI: Baker with the Calvin Institute of Christian Worship and Faith Alive Christian Resources, 2004
* Christopher Ellis and Myra Blyth, *Gathering for Worship: Patterns and Prayers for the Community of Disciples*, Norwich: Canterbury Press, 2005
Terry C. Falla, *Be our Freedom Lord: Responsive Prayers and Readings for Contemporary Worship*, Adelaide, Australia: Openbook Publishers, 1994
Morley, Janet, *Bread of Tomorrow: Praying with the World's Poor*, London: SPCK and Christian Aid, 1992

*J. Pritchard, *The Intercessions Handbook: Creative Ideas for Public and Private Prayer*, London: SPCK, 2008
*The SPCK Book of Christian Prayer*, London: SPCK, 1995

*And from the Iona Community:*

*The Iona Abbey Worship Book*, Glasgow: Wild Goose Publications, 2005
*A Wee Worship Book: Fourth Incarnation*, Glasgow: Wild Goose Publications, 1999
Kathy Galloway, *The Pattern of our Days: Liturgies and Resources for Worship*, Glasgow: Wild Goose Publications, 1996

## Singing

*J. L. Bell, *The Singing Thing: A Case for Congregational Song*, Glasgow: Wild Goose Publications, 2000
A. Maries, *One Heart, One Voice: The rich and varied resources of music in worship*, London: Hodder & Stoughton, 1985
B. Wren, *Praying Twice: The Music and Words of Congregational Song*, Louisville, KN: Westminster John Knox, 2000

There are so many sources for hymns and worship songs that it is difficult to know where to begin. Visit your local Christian bookshop and you will be spoilt for choice with both books of music and CDs. *Spring Harvest* produces an annual collection of contemporary songs as do other Christian gatherings. Often people get to know about new songs through the networking of local churches and Christian conferences, so I will leave you to do the networking . . .

Two very good introductions to traditional hymns are:

E. Routley and P. A. Richardson, *A Panorama of Christian Hymnody (Expanded Edition)*, Chicago, IL: GIA, 2005
J. R. Watson, *An Annotated Anthology of Hymns*, Oxford: Oxford University Press, 2002

## Scripture and Preaching

Fred B. Craddock, *Preaching*, Nashville, TN: Abingdon, 1985
*D. Day, *A Preaching Workbook*, London: Lynx/SPCK, 1998
M. B. Elliott, *Creative Styles of Preaching*, Louisville, KN: Westminster John Knox, 2000
N. Fawcett, *No Ordinary Man: Resources for Reflective Worship on the Person of Christ*, Bury St Edmunds: Kevin Mayhew, 1997
E. Lowry, *The Homiletical Plot: The Sermon as Narrative Art Form (Expanded Edition)*, Louisville, KN: Westminster John Knox, 2000
*P. S. Wilson, *The Four Pages of the Sermon: A Guide to Biblical Preaching*, Nashville, TN: Abingdon, 1999

## Celebrating

E. Kreider, *Given for You: Communion Past and Present*, Downers Grove, IL: InterVarsity Press, 1998

Pete Ward, *The Rite Stuff: Ritual in Contemporary Christian Worship and Mission*, Oxford: Bible Reading Fellowship, 2004

See also Ellis and Blyth, *Gathering for Worship: Patterns and Prayers for the Community of Disciples* (listed under 'Praying' above) which has a variety of communion services for free church use.

## Wider Horizons

P. Basden, *The Worship Maze: Finding a Style to Fit your Church*, Downers Grove, IL: InterVarsity Press, 1999

Paul Basden, *Exploring the Worship Spectrum*, Grand Rapids, MI: Zondervan, 2004

H. M. Best, *Unceasing Worship: Biblical Perspectives on Worship and the Arts*, Downers Grove, IL: InterVarsity Press, 2003

P. Craig-Wild, *Tools for Transformation: Making Worship Work*, London: Darton, Longman & Todd, 2002

M. Earey, *Liturgical Worship: A fresh look how it works, why it matters*, London: Church House Publishing, 2002

R. Redman, *The Great Worship Awakening: Singing a New Song in the Postmodern Church*, San Francisco, CA: Jossey-Bass/Wiley, 2002

*R. E. Webber, *Blended Worship: Achieving Substance and Relevance in Worship*, Peabody, MA: Hendrickson, 1994

## Time and Eternity

R. E. Webber, *Ancient-Future Time: Forming Spirituality through the Christian Year*, Grand Rapids, MI: Baker, 2004

## Reflecting

P. F. Bradshaw, *Two Ways of Praying: Introducing Liturgical Spirituality*, London: SPCK, 1995

R. Parry, *Worshiping Trinity: Coming Back to the Heart of Worship*, Bletchley: Paternoster, 2005

R. E. Webber, *Ancient-Future Faith: Rethinking Evangelicalism for a Postmodern World*, Grand Rapids, MI: Baker, 1999

R. Williams, *Tokens of Trust: An Introduction to Christian Belief*, Norwich: Canterbury Press, 2007

## Exploring the Web

For information about a general copyright license, look on the CCL website. But remember not all publishers and songs are covered:

http://www.ccli.co.uk/main.cfm

Here is a small selection of sites which offer either resources for, or reflections on, worship. I am sure you will find many more once you start looking.

http://bradberglund.com/

http://www.calvin.edu/worship/

http://divinity.library.vanderbilt.edu/lectionary/

http://www.gbod.org/worship/lectionary/

http://hymnal.oremus.org/hwiki/index.php/Main_Page

http://intercessions.co.uk/index.php/Main_Page

http://www.laughingbird.net/html/home.php

http://www.montreal.anglican.org/comments/

http://www.multisensoryworship.com/

# Sources and Acknowledgements

# Index of Names and Subjects

# Index of Scripture References